the new
I Ching

LILLIAN TOO

the new
I Ching

discover the secrets of
the plum blossom oracle

hamlyn

First published in Great Britain in 2004 by

Hamlyn, a division of Octopus Publishing Group Ltd

2–4 Heron Quays, London E14 4JP

Copyright © Octopus Publishing Group Ltd 2004

Text copyright © Lillian Too 2004

Distributed in the United States and Canada by

Sterling Publishing Co., Inc.

387 Park Avenue South, New York, NY 10016-8810

ISBN 0 600 60917 0

EAN 9780600609179

A CIP catalogue record for this book is available from the

British Library

Printed and bound in China

10 9 8 7 6 5 4 3 2 1

Contents

Introduction

To start new ventures, get married or make fresh commitments at the wrong time can be disastrous. It is better to check with the I Ching – the ancient Chinese book of divination – before taking any significant action that will have a long-term effect on your life. The I Ching is a gentle teacher – never dogmatic and rarely negative – and accessing it through the Plum Blossom Oracle will really enhance your awareness of the world around you and make you appreciate the importance of correct timing.

The Plum Blossom Oracle is as accurate when discussing your personal life as when sharing insights about events on the wider economic or world stage. I have used it repeatedly to assist me in making decisions for as long as I can remember. You will discover, as I did, that the oracle's reach is awesome and its accuracy improves each time you use it. It works by analysing the relationships between the trigrams that make up the hexagrams of the I Ching and using the texts of the hexagrams to open pathways into your intuitive mind. You will find yourself able to perceive things you would previously have missed and learn how to interpret what you see and sense.

The benefits of mastering the oracle are exciting beyond belief. Your judgment will improve, so you will be able to make decisions with greater clarity and firmness. Your assessment of probabilities will become sharper and your ability to evaluate situations will be enhanced because you will be able to see the bigger picture.

Once you have become attuned to the material and spiritual forces that impact on your well-being, you will start to live in a state of heightened awareness, alert to changes in the energy of your surroundings. For example, where before you might have been blind to signals from the cosmic universe – whether communicated through physical objects, people you meet or natural phenomena – now you will be aware of them.

At a personal level you will begin to see everything that happens – good and bad, positive and negative – as part of a grand design. It may be beyond your immediate comprehension but it will become clear later, perhaps years later, and you will come to understand that nothing is merely a coincidence.

So, observe what is happening around you. Look at your watch and note the time when something catches your eye. The very fact that you were drawn to pick up this book and read about the Plum Blossom Oracle is significant. It may well be steering you towards something important, perhaps something (or someone) heralding a new phase in your life …

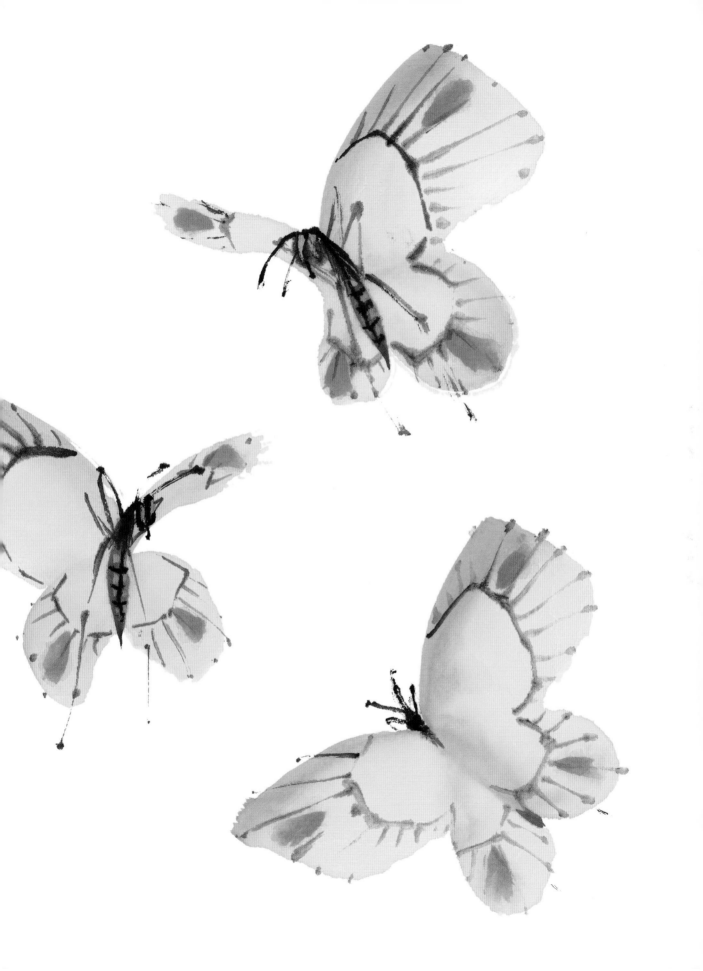

CHAPTER 1
Understanding the I Ching

Think of the I Ching as China's accumulated wisdom and philosophy encapsulated within a set of 64 linear symbols known as hexagrams. These lined symbols describe situations experienced by mankind working together with the forces of the universe. These forces are described by the Chinese as the interaction of tien ti ren, or heaven, earth and mankind.

What is the I Ching?

The I Ching or *Book of Changes*, China's oldest classical text and greatest sourcebook, is also the most famous oracle from ancient times to have survived intact into the twenty-first century. China was no different from many other countries in that oracles and divination played a significant part in her early history, exerting tremendous influence on the course of events. There are records from the Tang and Sung dynasties (618–907, 960–1279) of emperors and generals consulting the I Ching, while scholars who were expert in interpreting its advice on strategy and the timing of important edicts and attacks on enemies were highly valued members of the ruling elite. The I Ching was also used to assist in important decisions which affected the whole country. Today, although it has lost its exalted status at the court of rulers, it continues to be incredibly influential among the general population.

If you believe in oracles then you believe that the success of all your plans ultimately depends on the correct timing. When the timing is right a positive outcome is likely, because your actions – and equally your decisions not to act – will flow with the tide of chi. Chi is the life force or intangible energy that pervades the universe.

For years the I Ching has been a revered guide to perfect timing. It is fundamentally a book of symbols, which are categorized and ordered into sets of outcomes, attitudes and emotions. It does not offer life readings for individuals or specific prophecy; it is first and foremost an oracle.

The Chinese set great store by auspicious and inauspicious hours, days, months and years, believing that these are what determine the success of any undertaking. In fact, auspicious timing often seems to be more crucial than any action taken, so it has a fundamental part to play in using the I Ching. However, the texts also consider what action is appropriate: when to move ahead, when to wait and when to back off.

Any kind of question can be put to the I Ching for advice, comment and recommendations. At a personal level you can ask about marital prospects and the probable outcome of a particular match. You can also consult about your career: whether you will be promoted, should move job, can trust a new colleague and so on. If someone you care for is sick, you can ask if they will recover.

As an oracle the I Ching offers interpretations of great wisdom that will provide a guide at each moment in time and each stage in your life. It will help you to identify what will be significant turning points and tell you more about them, drawing attention to people around you and situations confronting you. It can be regarded as a friend, there to cheer, comfort and inspire you; or rather as an invisible friend – your higher self – given voice.

You will find that the texts of the I Ching contain words that seem to be exactly what you need to hear at the particular time of your consultation. The advice given is specific to the situation at any moment in time for whoever is asking, so it is seldom absolute.

This means that the I Ching can be referred to again and again. It is also possible to have a discussion with it, moving from one question to the next as you seek clarification. If you still do not quite understand the answer given, you can always rephrase your question.

The more serious you are in your approach and the more concentrated your frame of mind when constructing your questions, the more accurate and precise the answers will be. Successful consultations are often preceded by a heightened awareness of your surroundings and proceed from a keen mind, so make sure your environment is tranquil and relaxed. Also spend some moments reflecting on your question before asking it.

Irrespective of the different ways individuals think and their different circumstances, the I Ching can respond directly to every question asked. So whether you have a stunningly logical mind or are the sort of person who is sentimental, reaching decisions via the heart rather than the head, it will provide a source of personalized inner wisdom.

The I Ching is timeless in its appeal. If you use it often enough you will discover its immense pragmatism and the relevance it has to contemporary life. You will also realize, as you meditate on the responses it gives, that its words can lead you into new ways of thinking.

The I Ching or *Book of Changes*

The I Ching is neither a book of destiny nor a fortune-telling book that describes the fate of an individual. Consulting the I Ching is completely different from reading your Four Pillars of Destiny or using Purple Star astrology.* Those two methods create a road map of your fortunes in life. The I Ching does not describe a person's fate from birth to death, detailing the arrival of turning points such as the attaining of wealth or positions of power; nor does it foretell if someone will become rich or poor. Instead it is an oracle: it accesses your inner wisdom and helps you to interpret the signals contained in everyday experiences, encounters, sightings and phenomena.

* The Four Pillars of Destiny is a Chinese system of predicting life and destiny, while Purple Star astrology is a Chinese system of fortune-telling.

How to use the I Ching

To use the I Ching you need to know about hexagrams, the 64 symbols through which the oracle communicates. Hexagrams comprise two three-lined trigrams, one placed above the other. I Ching consultation involves the creation of the correct hexagram for your question. In order to interpret a hexagram, it is necessary to understand its root trigrams as well as its texts, judgments and commentaries.

All this can sound rather complex, but once you start to use it the oracle will take on a life and a charm of its own, seducing you into exploring the inner recesses of your mind. With practice, you will be dazzled by your ability to interpret the trigrams as they interact and tell their stories. Eventually you will find yourself able to anticipate the outcome of decisions, events and actions with increasing accuracy. The oracle will help you confirm negative or positive feelings about new people who come into your life. It will hone your analysis of propositions, improve your confidence and enhance your decision-making skills. In time you will come to realize that it can give advice on just about anything.

Learning the oracle is an education in itself. You will discover that it contains different dimensions of meaning that encompass the esoteric components of life – numerology, astrology and their impact on the elements that make up the universe. It respects the

yin (negative, silent and stagnant) and yang (positive, active and moving) aspects of tai chi (the circular yin and yang symbol). It considers the positive and negative manifestations of the five elements (see page 33). It takes account of the weather, the strength of the winds, the shape of the clouds, the brightness of the sunshine and the wetness of the day. In short, it embraces everything that occurs, and then interprets it through the hexagram constructed.

Every reading will deepen your understanding of the situation being analysed. You will find that interpreting the oracle becomes a deeply personal and creative exercise. At first you can use the texts and interpretations in this book to assist you, but over time the images, symbols and commentaries that are a part of each hexagram's attributes will begin to suggest other connections to you. It is then that you will realize how observant of the world you have become, and this in itself will hone your sensitivity to the energy around you.

Do note, however, that if you ask silly questions and keep repeating yourself, you are treating the oracle with disrespect and it will give you frivolous replies that seem to have nothing to do with what you are asking. Sometimes it will even chide you, although at other times it will laugh along with you.

Respect the I Ching

As an oracle technique, the I Ching is viewed by some as an exploration of the unconscious mind – an investigation into the subconscious wisdom that resides within the human psyche. Scholars who have studied the detailed texts of the I Ching are at pains to stress that it must never be treated as frivolous superstition. Indeed, those who consult this classic know how important it is to treat it with respect and even reverence.

The Trigrams

A trigram is a figure made up of three lines, and these lines can be either unbroken (yang) or broken (yin). The lines signify the two basic forces of the physical world, the creative, strong, masculine yang energy and the receptive, yielding, feminine yin energy. The wisdom of yang and the compassion of yin unite to produce an infinite number of outcomes.

Yin and yang feature prominently in the I Ching. The trigrams are arranged in two sequences that make up the yin and yang pa kua (an eight-sided symbol used in Feng Shui analysis). These two arrangements contain the key to unlocking the precious secrets of the inner mind and find expression through the hexagrams of the I Ching.

Trigrams feature in a similar way in Feng Shui, the Chinese system that advocates living in harmony with one's environment in order to enhance wealth, health and happiness luck. Understanding trigrams gives anyone a competitive edge in the predictive, divinitive and Feng Shui practices of China.

There are eight trigrams: Chien, Kun, Chen, Sun, Tui, Ken, Kan and Li. Collectively they symbolize a trinity of world principles recognized as heaven, earth and mankind. The Chinese identify three types of luck: heaven luck (tien chai), earth luck (ti chai) and mankind luck (ren chai).

Heaven luck is what you are born with. To get an idea of what heaven has destined for you, consult a fortune-teller well versed in the Four Pillars method or the Purple Star system of astrology. Remember, however, that heaven luck is sweeping and broad-based; what is more, it is only a third of your luck. While it is not within your control and is impossible to change, your destiny can be improved by creating good mankind luck and positive earth luck.

Earth luck is generally referred to as Feng Shui luck: that is, living in harmony with the chi of the earth's environment. It also represents human interaction with their surroundings – whether such interaction brings good fortune or bad – and complements heaven luck.

Mankind luck refers to your conduct, action, attitude, judgment, skills and so on. The I Ching is here to help you live your life in a way that maximizes this luck. The 'superior man' referred to in the texts of the I Ching is one who understands the three-dimensional concept symbolized by the trigrams, each of which has its own multiple sets of meaning, symbols and connotations. The 'superior man' in this context refers to both genders.

The eight trigrams symbolize many things: numbers, colours, shapes, seasons, compass directions, abstract feelings, one of the five elements, one of the organs of the body, a family member, one of the celestial creatures – the list is endless. In a trigram the bottom line represents earth, the middle line represents mankind and the upper line represents heaven. In order to understand the trigrams, it is necessary to focus on their major attributes.

Chien

This is the Creative and it comprises three unbroken solid lines, indicating strength, power and endurance. It is the ultimate yang trigram and is associated with the father, the patriarch and the male paternal. It also signifies the leader, heaven, the sky, celestial spheres, activity, power, brightness, bright colours, energy and perseverance. Chien has more positive than negative attributes. If there is a negative, it is that there could be an excess of yang energy, suggesting over-activity, extreme enthusiasm and too much zeal or passion.

The element of Chien is big metal and its symbolic animal is the horse, denoting power, endurance, firmness and strength. Here the horse is the victory horse who outruns all others, even the swiftest swallow. Chien is thus a signal that means victory.

Chien is the most positive of the trigrams. It also suggests a purity and firmness of motive. Chien indicates circular objects, spheres, crystal balls, rounded edges and circular motifs. In terms of body parts, Chien represents the head, the mind and brainpower, thus indicating mental superiority.

How Chien interacts with other trigrams depends on the elements of those it is paired with. Whether the message is positive or negative depends on whether Chien is the upper or lower trigram.

In terms of direction, Chien signifies south in the Early Heaven arrangement of trigrams (see page 41) and north-west in the Later Heaven arrangement (see pages 51). Its number depends on which arrangement of trigrams is being used.

Chien doubled forms the first hexagram of the I Ching, whose power is strong and creative. If you obtain this hexagram in reply to a query then you are being told, 'Heaven is helping', a creative force is lending a hand. It also suggests the presence of a strong, invisible mentor-like figure watching over you. This hexagram is indicative of ultimate good fortune and a successful outcome. It suggests the vanquishing of opponents, victory in a righteous fight and overcoming the competition.

Kun

This is the Receptive and is made up of three broken yin lines. These lines together represent the dark, yielding and primal power of yin. The attributes of this trigram refer to the mother, the female, maternal power and matriarchal chi. It signifies the caring of a devoted mother and its image is big earth. Warm, caring and friendly Kun is the perfect partner of Chien, the Creative, because the Receptive does not fight with the Creative, but completes it.

Kun's animal is the cow, with a calf thereby symbolizing family, fertility, docility and submission. Kun signifies nature in contrast to heaven, female in contrast to male, and space against time. For purposes of prediction, the interpretation of Kun refers not only to the prince and minister relationship but also to the father and son, husband and wife, employer and employee, with Kun always representing the subordinate and Chien the leader. In terms of body parts, Kun signifies the stomach and the womb, organs related to nurturing and procreation. Kun is therefore symbolic of ultimate survival, fertility and continuity.

For Feng Shui the direction under the Early Heaven arrangement is north and, under the Later Heaven arrangement, south-west.

Kun doubled forms the mother hexagram of the I Ching, whose power is strong but yielding. If you obtain this hexagram in reply to a query then you are being reminded of the vast benefits that are associated with giving in: that is, in apparent yielding lies strength and the potential for triumph. It suggests the presence of a benevolent mother-like figure watching over you. Kun is also a hexagram that indicates the ultimate triumph of the mother energy, which is strong enough to overcome adversity, setbacks and loss.

Chen

This signifies the Arousing and is made up of two broken yin lines above one solid yang line. The trigram represents the eldest son and is often associated with movement and decision-making, vehemence and shock. Its image is thunder and it is symbolized by the dragon, which arises from the depths, soars magnificently up into the stormy skies and flies in fearsome frolic. With the single strong yang line pushing upward below two yielding yin lines, this trigram signifies growth and a thrusting upward and outward.

Chen's colour is dark yellow, suggesting spring's luxuriant growth, which covers the earth with plants. Chen's element is big wood. When combined with its productive element (see page 36), Chen signifies abundant growth and quick success. When combined with a metal element, it becomes hurt and signifies danger. When combined with fire, it is exhausted.

This trigram always advises caution, which brings good fortune. It suggests inner calm in the midst of a storm, a man who makes himself respected by being careful and exact to the smallest detail. Its direction in the Early Heaven arrangement is north-east and in the Later Heaven arrangement east.

Sun

This signifies the Penetrating and is made up of two solid yang lines above a single broken yin line. The trigram represents the eldest daughter and signifies the wind, which can be gentle or strong. Since it also manifests the strength that comes from being gentle, the wind here blows wealth and riches, especially when combined with the element of water. But when the wind turns fierce and strong, it can bring chaos and storms. This sometimes happens when it is combined with the fire element.

Sun represents small wood, which, in terms of outcomes, signifies a time of indecision. Its celestial creature is the rooster, whose voice pierces the still morning air. In this context, the rooster is a bird of opportunity, responsibility and also fierce protectiveness in the face of adversity. Reliability is suggested too, for the rooster is capable of both taking flight and holding its ground, fighting to the end.

Among men, Sun signifies those with broad foreheads and much white in their eyes. It predicts the making of profits, so those who get this trigram can expect to obtain threefold value. Sun is sometimes a sign of vehemence. Its direction in the Early Heaven arrangement is south-west and in the Later Heaven arrangement south-east.

Tui

This signifies the Joyous and is made up of one broken yin line above two solid yang lines. Tui represents a celebration of some kind, meaning merry-making and happiness.

Tui indicates the youngest daughter or any young girl who brings happiness. When this trigram is placed above and represents the subject matter of any consultation, it always suggests the importance of a young woman in the situation.

Tui is the beautiful lake and the wet marshlands as well. The lake contains many unknown things and is also a mirror to reflect all your innermost thoughts. Sometimes it can suggest excessive worrying. This trigram advocates turning away from worry and rejoicing instead in the knowledge of just living. Its element is small metal.

Tui is also the mouth through which mankind eats, speaks and breathes, creating joy for themselves and for others. But the mouth can cause problems as well, since it suggests gossip and loose talk. This is because Tui means the concubine syndrome, a lover, a petite woman too – a person who appears outwardly weak but is inwardly stubborn. Tui can also suggest a conniving female with a dangerous hidden agenda. It is associated with autumn, a time of falling leaves prior to hibernation. Its direction in the Early Heaven arrangement is south-east and in the Later Heaven arrangement west.

When combined with fire, Tui either gets destroyed or goes on to greater strength. When combined with water, it is exhausted. When combined with earth, it flourishes.

Ken

This signifies the image of the Mountain and comprises a solid yang line above two broken yin lines. The symbolism here is of great strength keeping silent and still – hiding many things within its core.

Ken represents the youngest son in the family. Its meaning suggests that there is much mystery and hidden expectations. It confirms that there are unspoken motives in relationships and new meetings and it urges caution. The outcome is usually too deeply buried to surface immediately.

Ken has been likened to a final stage of life and the promise of a new beginning. Life, death and resurrection – these are prompted by the transition of an old to a new year. Ken thus sometimes signifies a time of solitude, reflection and waiting. It advises to do nothing, to keep still and to take time off for study and reflection. It is the link between an ending and a beginning.

The element of Ken is small earth. Its direction in the Early Heaven arrangement is north-west and in the Later Heaven arrangement north-east. When combined with fire, it blossoms and comes alive with new strength and vigour. When combined with a wood trigram, it signifies unhappy endings. When combined with a metal trigram, it suggests a serious weakening of a situation.

Kan

This signifies the Abysmal and is often regarded as a danger trigram. It is made up of one solid yang line sandwiched between two broken yin lines – life being kept imprisoned by death!

Kan strongly represents danger, so the connotations of this trigram have to do with warnings of all kinds. It usually signifies hardship, toil and, when combined with wood trigrams, melancholia. The trigram itself symbolizes sadness because two weak lines are constraining one strong line. Many masters interpret this as indicating difficulties and hard work.

Since its element is water, the potential for positive or negative outcomes is considered to be more extreme than with other trigrams. Water can bring a massive flow of extra income but it can also suggest death from overflowing. Water can sustain as well as drown you! The other element of danger is fire, which can either bring you a great deal of positive recognition or burn you when it is out of control. So, like fire, water is best when properly controlled.

Kan represents the middle son and its season is winter. It further signifies the pearl and also meeting up with someone who is crafty, someone you must be very careful of, because there will be hidden agendas causing confusion and misfortune. Its direction in the Early Heaven arrangement is west and in the Later Heaven arrangement north.

Li

This signifies the Clinging, made up of one weak broken line hemmed in by two solid yang lines. Li is fire, the sun, brightness, lightning, heat and warmth.

The character of the trigram suggests something firm on the outside but weak, hollow, yielding and docile inside. Like fire, which eventually burns itself out, leaving nothing in its wake, Li suggests short-lived success. It is also like lightning: bright light for an instant but then it is gone. Sometimes this is interpreted to mean a person with no substance despite a glamorous exterior. At other times it can suggest a plan with very little or no chance of long-term success due to lack of real substance.

Li is also the middle daughter and the trigram strongly suggests dependence, although of a kind that is positive and nourishing, as when a plant clings to the soil and grows. In the predictive sense, this trigram suggests potential, as symbolized by the brightness aspect. Indeed Li can set the world on fire, but it will have to work hard to do so. It represents warmth and the summer sun which illuminates all things. Its direction in the Early Heaven arrangement is east and in the Later Heaven arrangement south.

When combined with water, Li loses some of its lustre, for water puts out fire, but when water is weak and fire dominates what is produced could turn into enormous power. Li also comes into its own and indicates continued success when it combines with wood. This is because wood fuels fire, keeping the flames alight and burning steadily.

The Different Methods of Consulting the I Ching

This book concentrates on the Plum Blossom Oracle, but there are several ways to construct the hexagrams of the I Ching. You can, for example, use coins, yarrow stalks or bamboo sticks. Each of these represents a different method of I Ching divination and has special attributes that will appeal to different people. Selecting which approach to use is very much a matter of personal preference.

All the approaches date back to ancient times, when the Chinese first devised methods for determining hexagrams which would contain a description of the situation as well as offer advice based on possible outcomes to questions asked. Two major systems were extremely popular. The first was a symbolic technique involving the use of a tortoise shell, while the second was numerical and required making calculations with yarrow stalks.

These methods were difficult and time-consuming. In the latter part of the Chou dynasty (403–221 BCE), about eighty years after the death of Confucius, a divination method involving the use of coins was invented by the great hermit philosopher and military strategist Kuei Kuo Tse. Widely revered as a mysterious sage, Kuei had hundreds of statesmen,

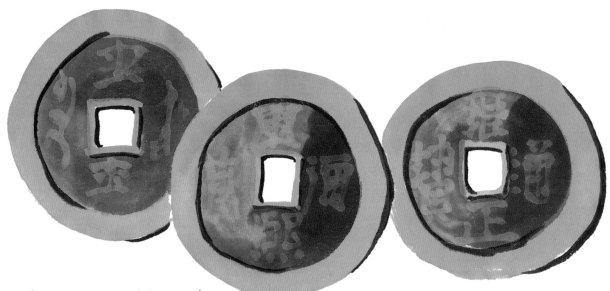

military men, magicians and astrologers studying under him in the mountains. He deemed the old methods too cumbersome, especially during the turbulent times of the warring states, so he invented the Coin Oracle, a method of divination that would eventually supersede all earlier forms.

The Coin Oracle is still widely used in Chinese society, but there have always been variations in the actual throwing of the coins and the number of coins used. Some people use only one to obtain simple yes/no or good/bad responses, while others prefer the use of three, six, eight or even 16 coins to construct the relevant predictive hexagram.

Historically, those who regularly consulted the I Ching preferred to use the three-coin method and from the seventeenth century onwards this version of the 'Coin Oracle as refined by the scholar Wang Hung Shu' became very popular. It uses the tossing of three coins to construct the predictive hexagrams and is briefly described here for two main reasons: first, because it is the form of consultation most people in the West are familiar with; and second, because you may well wish to use it to complement the Plum Blossom method.

The Coin Oracle

Serious practitioners of the Coin Oracle prefer to use ancient Chinese coins, but well-made copies are also acceptable and are not difficult to obtain. It might be an idea to look for Chinese coins from the nine prosperous dynasties – a period of peace and prosperity – as they would be auspicious. These old coins are round with a square hole in the centre. The round shape symbolizes heaven (signified by the trigram Chien), while the square hole stands for earth (signified by the trigram Kun).

The yang or positive side usually has four characters written in Chinese with the meaning 'your luck has arrived'. The yin or negative side has two characters and these, added to the four characters of the yang side, make six characters, which are said to reflect the six lines of the hexagrams. The use of three coins symbolizes the trinity of earth, man and heaven, and also the three lines of the trigrams. Using six coins reflects the influence of heaven luck.

If old coins are not available it is perfectly acceptable to use normal everyday coins. Heads stand for yang positive, while tails stand for yin negative.

Selecting and Preparing the Coins

If you want to practise the Coin Oracle seriously, you should buy six coins and make two sets, which you should always look after with great care. Select coins that 'feel right' in your hands, so spend a few minutes tuning in to them. Do not allow the shop assistant to hurry you. In fact, when you are buying any divination product always ensure that your frame of mind is happy and relaxed. If you feel annoyed for any reason postpone your purchase.

It is the symbolism of the coins rather than their age that gives them power. If you want to buy genuine antique coins, make sure they come from a good source. Coins from rich mansions or the tombs of successful dynasties, palaces and banks are said to possess wealth energy. Personally I prefer modern copies, but that is only because I am always wary of the 'history' of objects. Who knows what kind of unhappiness energy clings to old coins?

When you have purchased your coins, buy a small container to keep them in, preferably one made of lacquer and lined with velvet or silk. First, you must 'purify' your coins in order to get rid of any negative energy that may still be clinging to them. Give them a good scrub and then allow them to sit in the sun for three hours a day for seven consecutive days. Sunlight not only purifies the coins and rids them of dead chi but also activates their intrinsic symbolic essence, which is a medium for obtaining all the material goods in the world. Because this energy is so strong and powerful, the older and more used the coins are the better. Coins that have been empowered with the brilliant yang energy of the sun are said to have come alive.

It is advisable to set these three coins aside for frequent use so that over time they become closely associated with you and your I Ching consultations. The coins should be kept carefully wrapped up in velvet and stored away in the box when they are not in use.

If you wish, you can also imbue your coins with yin energy. Do this by letting them sit in moonlight over seven consecutive nights, but make sure you avoid a waning moon, as this will deplete their energy and deprive them of their strength.

Tossing the Coins

Before tossing the coins to consult the I Ching for predictions, calm your mind and focus inwards. Think through the various aspects of the dilemma about which you are seeking advice and guidance. I almost always make a great ritual out of my consultation sessions. I prefer the early hours of the morning, when the world is still asleep and the energy is pure and silent. I usually consult the I Ching after my pre-dawn meditation, when my mind is at its clearest – rested after a good night's sleep and refreshed by the meditation.

Take out your coins and lay them on a red velvet cloth. If you do not have velvet, use silk instead. When you are ready, place the coins in a container (a metal one is best) and shake them vigorously. You could shake the coins in your hand but this is not as efficient. While shaking, concentrate on your question and ask for a clear, easy-to-understand answer. Now toss the coins on to the velvet.

You will have to toss the three coins six times in order to obtain the six lines of the hexagram. After each throw, which represents one line of the hexagram, analyse how the coins fall.

Constructing the Hexagram

The hexagram is constructed from the bottom up, so the first throw determines the first, bottom line, and you build up from there. Each time the coins fall there are four possible combinations:

- **young yang** (one yang, two yin) represents an unchanging solid yang line;

- **young yin** (one yin, two yang) represents an unchanging broken yin line;

- **old yang** (three yang) represents a changing solid yang line;

- **old yin** (three yin) represents a changing broken yin line.

Construct the hexagram accordingly. Here is what a typical hexagram resulting from tossing the coins might look like (see below):

Changing Lines

Each time the coins fall and display either three yang or three yin sides, the particular line represented is referred to as a changing line. These lines may change from broken to unbroken or vice versa. Whenever changing lines are indicated, three things should be noted:

- If the changing line is solid it changes to a broken line. If the changing line is broken it changes to a solid line. Thus a yang line always changes to a yin line and vice versa.

- A new hexagram is formed, so there are now two hexagrams that answer your question. The first hexagram describes the situation, while the second describes the outcome.

- The changing lines themselves indicate the prediction of the first hexagram. For example, if the third line is a changing line, read the prediction represented by the third line. If there is more than one changing line, read all the predictions indicated and try to formulate a pattern to the message being given.

Mark all your changing lines with a cross or asterisk.

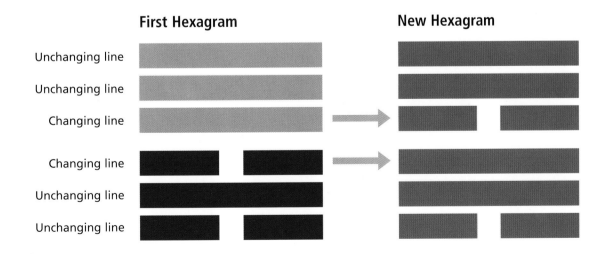

First Hexagram		New Hexagram

Unchanging line		
Unchanging line		
Changing line	→	
Changing line	→	
Unchanging line		
Unchanging line		

CHAPTER 2
The Plum Blossom Oracle

The Chinese cherish plum blossom for its almost celestial significance. Each season, despite the most intense cold, thousands of exquisite blooms burst forth from twisted, rough and gnarled branches, manifesting cosmic resilience during a barren time, sending out the happy signal that spring is just around the corner. The plum tree has great and auspicious meaning. Flowering after the frosts, it symbolizes hope and endurance. As the tree awakes from its winter sleep, slender bold shoots thrust themselves into existence, and this signifies the audacity of youth amidst the accumulated wisdom represented by the older, wrinkled and twisted branches.

The Origins of the Plum Blossom Oracle

At some time during the early years of the Sung dynasty, a small group of philosophers proposed a synthesis of Confucianism, Taoism and Buddhism, the three great ideas of China that had been competing for supremacy.

One member of this group was a scholar named Shao Kang Chieh, who, with his contemporaries, was to inspire a Neo-Confucian tradition that would eventually come to dominate Chinese thinking for ten centuries. Shao is best remembered for his brilliant commentaries on the I Ching and his incorporation of numerology and observed phenomena into the consultation process. He based his method on secret instructions that had come into his possession in mysterious circumstances.

On a hot afternoon, while Shao was taking a nap, a rat disturbed his sleep. On awakening, he accidentally knocked his ceramic pillow to the floor. Looking at the broken pieces, Shao discovered a note on which was written his name and a prediction of the exact time at which he would break the pillow. Intrigued, he immediately sought out the manufacturer of the pillow, only to discover that the man had died two days earlier. However, he had left behind a note, together with a thick package for 'the man who would come enquiring about the note in the pillow'.

When Shao opened the package, he discovered detailed notes on a unique way of formulating the hexagrams of the I Ching for consultation purposes. He realized that the method described resolved problems he had been struggling with for some time, confirming his belief in the importance of the influence of time.

One morning, when Shao was in his garden meditating, his attention was drawn to some plum blossom. He noticed two sparrows fighting in the branches of the tree and watched as the birds fell to the ground. Fascinated, he used the new method of consultation to create a hexagram of the I Ching that provided him with further insights. Incorporating the image of sparrows fighting amidst the plum blossom with the exact time of

the morning, he created the six-line hexagram that revealed the advice he was seeking. He was later astounded by the accuracy and wisdom of the I Ching's response as laid out in the hexagram and its moving lines. This explains why he called his system of I Ching divination the Plum Blossom Oracle.

Since Shao's time, the elite among Chinese I Ching scholars have rationalized the use of the Plum Blossom Oracle, placing more emphasis on the selection of observed phenomena to cast their hexagrams. Over the centuries the method has been successfully used to enhance understanding of chance encounters, significant events and the motives of

new acquaintances. Practitioners have discovered that incorporating the symbols and signs that materialize as everyday events, dreams or even unexpected encounters add greater depth to the readings.

How to Consult the Oracle

Two different methods, the Early Heaven and Later Heaven trigram arrangements, can be grouped under the broad heading the Plum Blossom Oracle. Both use simple trigram numerology to arrive at a base hexagram. With practice you will be able to select the one you prefer, depending mainly on your affinity with it, but also on what questions you wish to ask the I Ching.

The numbers assigned to the eight trigrams are different in the two arrangements, so each arrangement will yield a different hexagram. Whichever method you use, they both require the creation of a base hexagram which is then analysed on the basis of its four component trigrams: the outer, or primary, upper and lower trigrams and the upper and lower nuclear, or hidden, trigrams.

The lower primary trigram is made up of the first, second and third lines of the hexagram (counting from the bottom upwards).

The upper primary trigram is made up of the fourth, fifth and sixth lines of the hexagram.

The lower nuclear trigram is made up of the second, third and fourth lines of the hexagram (counting from the bottom upwards).

The upper nuclear trigram is made up of the third, fourth and fifth lines of the hexagram.

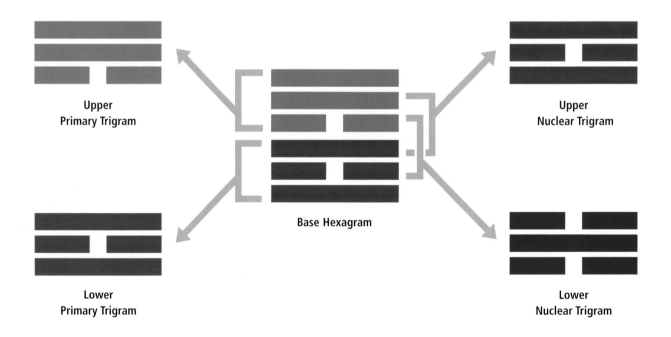

Upper Primary Trigram

Upper Nuclear Trigram

Base Hexagram

Lower Primary Trigram

Lower Nuclear Trigram

The Trigrams and the Five Elements

Every trigram has an element: metal, wood, earth, water or fire. Metal, wood and earth have a large and a small aspect to their chi and it is useful, when analysing the element relationships, to take note of this. They are said to be less volatile than the other two elements, fire and water, which cannot be stored, held or grasped. Fire and water are double-edged, bringing either massive misfortune or enormous good luck. Too much fire is incredibly dangerous but is also literally brilliant. Too much water is awesome in its power but also amazingly potent in the wealth it brings. It is important to bear these two extremes in mind when analysing hexagrams that contain either fire or water trigrams.

Chien and Tui: Metal

Chien is big metal and Tui small metal, so Chien would symbolize objects that are larger than Tui. Chien also stands for the father, the leader, heaven, the patron, the king, the general, the boss and the ultimate in yang energy. It is thus an activity trigram that is full of strong and powerful energy (Chien lines are described as strong). Tui, on the other hand, stands for young girl, who can be the youngest daughter, a concubine or a young maid. It also signifies the lake and a gentle disposition.

Kun and Ken: Earth

Kun is big earth – strong and powerfully yin – while Ken is small earth – the mountain. Kun stands for a mature woman, the matriarch, mother force, someone nurturing and caring. It is a yin trigram as powerful as Chien, although not overtly so. Ken signifies the youngest son, a boy still in need of his mother's care. Both the trigrams indicate a grounding quality that suggests stability, hidden power and knowledge. Earth trigrams always indicate steadfastness in any given situation, but also imply a need for patience.

Chen and Sun: Wood

Chen is big wood, while Sun is small wood. Chen stands for the eldest son. It can also represent an ambitious and spoilt young man, used to having his own way. It signifies a large, fast-growing tree and suggests impatience and vigorous activity. Sun signifies the eldest daughter, strong outside but filled with misgivings – a certain amount of insecurity and lack of confidence. It can also signify an older woman, a relative or an outsider.

Li: Fire

The trigram Li signifies fire, an element that does not exist of its own accord. Fire is an energy source that cannot be stored and must be created to exist. Yet when alight, fire can bring warmth and sustenance. Fire can be dangerous and at its zenith is as fierce and as unrelenting as water. In terms of aspirations and meanings the fire of the Li trigram brings recognition, fame and influence. When it is positive it brings popularity and when it is negative it brings notoriety and infamy.

Kan and Tui: Water

The trigram Kan stands for flowing water, while Tui represents a body of water. Kan is related to career achievements and signifies a flow of income. It manifests itself in two extremes: outstanding financial success and extreme danger. Tui is symbolized by a lake and suggests an accumulation of wealth, but it can also indicate a loss of wealth. Both trigrams indicate matters pertaining to earning capacity and all things material.

How the Trigrams Relate to Each Other

The way to analyse any hexagram is to see how the elements of its two primary and two nuclear trigrams interact. The relationship between the trigrams can be one of three kinds: productive, destructive or exhaustive. These are the three important cycles of relationships between the five elements. The arrows in the diagram below indicate the productive cycle; the diagram on page 37 shows the exhaustive cycle, while the diagram of the five pointed star on page 38 reveals the destructive cycle.

When the trigrams are in a productive relationship, this is auspicious and harmonious and so the indications are positive, suggesting expansion, growth and the arrival of good news. When the relationships are destructive or exhaustive, this indicates misfortune, failure and disharmony and thus can give rise for concern.

Destructive relationships are often indications of danger, so when the upper and lower trigrams indicate a destructive relationship this should immediately alert you to possible clues from the inner nuclear trigrams. Destructive relationships that

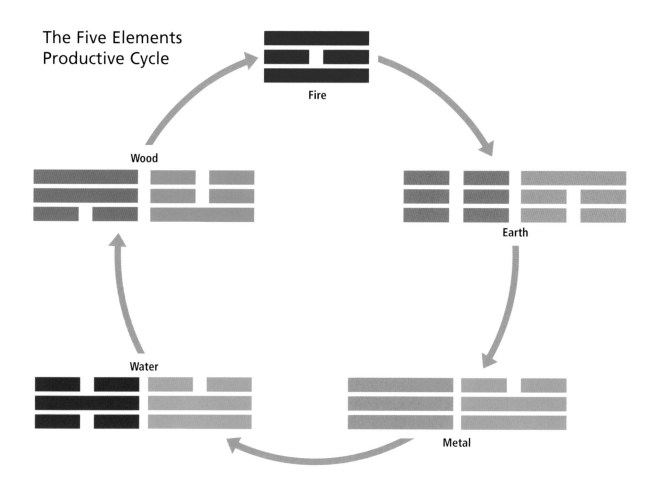

The Five Elements Productive Cycle

Fire

Wood

Earth

Water

Metal

involve the metal element always suggest some kind of violence. If fire is involved as well, then the indications are extremely dangerous, since fire is red and so is blood. Look at the elements and see what they suggest to you and how you can relate them to the question being asked. Study the diagram again and take note of the destructive relationships so you can spot them each time they appear.

Elements that are in an exhaustive relationship are less deadly but can also be dangerous long-term. It depends on which trigram (upper or lower) is exhausting which trigram. The key is to decide whether either of the trigrams is referring to you and then to see if the trigram that represents you is being exhausted. Usually the upper trigram is interpreted as the subject, so always check whether the element of the upper trigram is being destroyed or produced by the lower trigram. There is a third relationship and that is exhausting the subject. This too has relevance.

For example, if you are a middle-aged woman and the trigram Kun is one of the trigrams in the hexagram, you know you are represented. Note that the trigram Kun has earth as its element, so if the other trigram in the hexagram is Li it means that it is

The Five Elements Exhaustive Cycle

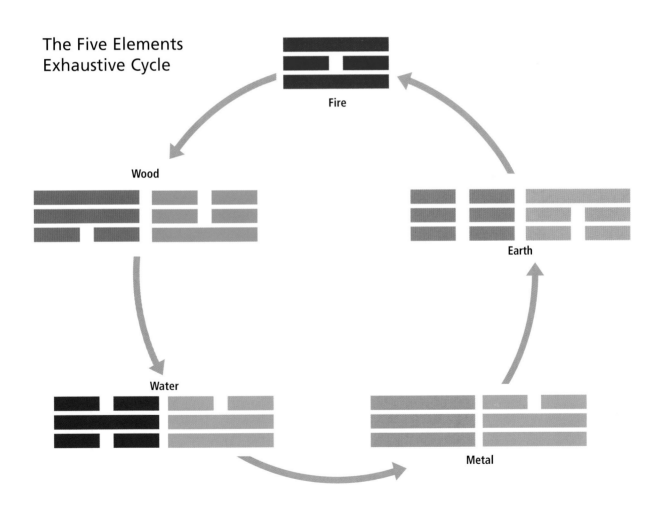

Fire

Wood

Earth

Water

Metal

exhausting you. Li stands for the middle daughter, but it also signifies another woman, perhaps someone younger, so a hexagram made up of Kun and Li suggests some kind of exhaustive relationship between two women.

Understanding the elements, their relationships and how to use them in analysing the hexagrams is a large part of what the Plum Blossom Oracle is about. Take another example. You are a young man asking about the outcome of a job interview and you obtain the hexagram Pi, which has Li as the lower primary trigram and Ken as the upper primary trigram (fire

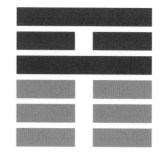

The hexagram Chin has Kun as the lower primary trigram and Li as the upper primary trigram.

below and earth above). Here the trigrams are indicating a productive cycle, since fire produces earth, so immediately you know that the hexagram is indicating good fortune.

The Five Elements Destructive Cycle

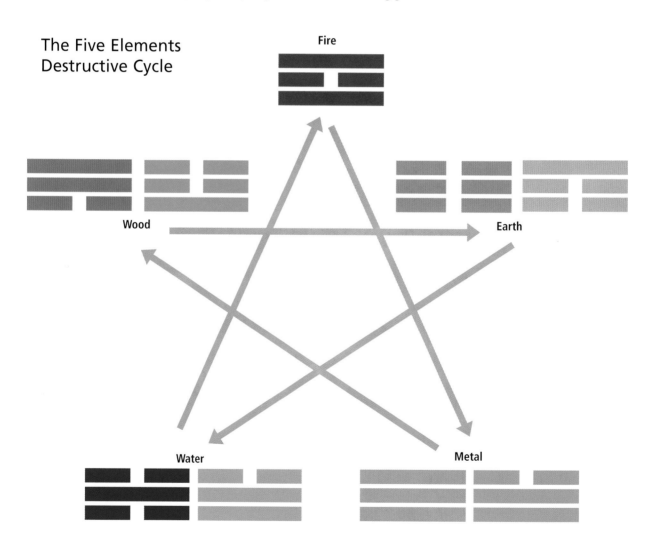

The hexagram Pi has Li as the lower primary trigram and Ken as the upper primary trigram.

Better still, as the trigram Ken stands for a young man and the person asking the question is a young man, it is an even more accurate indication. Why? Because Ken is the trigram being helped by the other trigram. If you then refer to the texts of the hexagram Pi (which also means gracefulness), you will discover that the symbolism here is of fire illuminating a mountain and making it beautiful. The hexagram is indicating a bright career ahead of this young man – in other words, the I Ching is saying that he will be successful and is advising him to take the job.

Once you have familiarized yourself with the elements and their relationships, you need to differentiate between the primary and the nuclear trigram relationships. Generally speaking, the former indicate external or immediate outcomes, while the latter offer hidden or longer-term meanings about a situation. These hidden meanings may or may not be immediately obvious but they do suggest a deeper perspective on the question asked. Usually it is not necessary to analyse the nuclear trigrams unless the question being asked is of vital long-term significance (if, for example, your time frame is more than a year).

The initial analysis of the element relationships of any hexagram is the same irrespective of the method used for creating the hexagram. It is therefore good to begin by becoming familiar with the different elements of the trigrams.

The Changing Line

Both methods of the Plum Blossom Oracle describe a way of determining the changing line which, through the I Ching texts, offers clues to the immediate outcome of the question asked (see Chapter 5 for full details). A changing solid line transforms into a broken line, while a changing broken line transforms into a solid line. More importantly, the changing line causes the base hexagram to transform into a predictive hexagram, which is what will give you the expected outcome to the question asked.

So to consult the oracle you must know how to create the base hexagram with the formula that will enable you to use numerology to convert observed phenomena and the exact time of occurrence first into trigrams and then into hexagrams.

Creating the Hexagram

Look on the two ways of creating hexagrams as two steps in learning the Plum Blossom Oracle. Both call for increasing use of your powers of observation to develop communication with the I Ching and, through it, your inner mind. This will be easier if you begin by using the Early Heaven arrangement of trigrams to familiarize yourself with the oracle's method and also to access the heaven dimension of the trinity of the cosmic universe.

Later on, when you progress to using the Later Heaven arrangement of trigrams, you will be accessing the other two dimensions of the trinity, earth and mankind. The former tends to deal with issues that are out of your control, while the latter deals with those more within your control. The two methods differ in the way the trigrams of the base hexagram are created and in the formulation of the changing line.

Early Heaven Trigram Arrangement Method

This uses the numbers assigned to the trigrams in the Early Heaven arrangement based on Fu Hsi's original arrangement. (Fu Hsi, the legendary first emperor of China, is the person who invented the I Ching.) It would be a good idea at this stage to learn the names of the trigrams and to note the numbers assigned to each of them in this arrangement.

The trigrams making up the hexagram are derived from the numbers created by the numerical aspects of the situation being investigated and the time of consultation. The two trigrams then make up the base hexagram. There will thus be an upper and a lower trigram.

The attributes of the trigrams play a significant part in the answers given, so, for a fuller picture of the advice of the I Ching, study the interactions of the elements represented by the two trigrams, which reveal both outcomes and predictions, and place less emphasis on the texts of the I Ching.

This method is preferred when investigating questions that involve 'timing' or a 'luck' element. It also suggests the supremacy of heaven in the trinity of heaven, mankind and earth.

Determining the Lower Trigram

The lower trigram is determined by using the exact time at which the consultation is taking place. This means that all four pillars of time – hour, day, month and year – must be incorporated into the calculation. Obviously, the I Ching is based on the Chinese lunar calendar. However, many masters agree that since we are now using the I Ching at a time when the Western calendar seems to be universally accepted, it is fine to use it to calculate the numerology of the trigram. If, however, you prefer to use the lunar calendar, you will have to convert your date to that of the Chinese lunar date. Personally, I do not see the need.

There are four steps to take when determining the lower trigram of your base hexagram:

1. Note the time. The Chinese divide the 24-hour day into 12 time segments, each of which has a corresponding number (see Table 1 on page 42). This is the number used to convert the time into a numerical aspect. Next take note of the date of the consultation. You will need this information to create the numerical aspect from which you then derive the lower trigram.

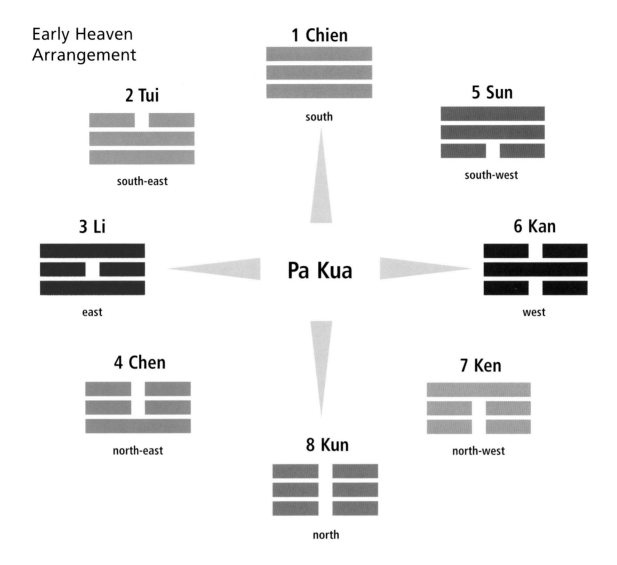

Early Heaven
Arrangement

1 Chien

south

2 Tui

south-east

5 Sun

south-west

3 Li

east

Pa Kua

6 Kan

west

4 Chen

north-east

7 Ken

north-west

8 Kun

north

2. Use Table 1 (see page 42) to find the numerical aspects of the hour, month, day and year. Add them together to reach your number.

3. If the total is 8 or less you have the number to determine the trigram. If not, divide the total by 8 and then use the remainder for your number. If the number is divisible by 8 then 8 is your number.

4. Determine the trigram that corresponds to this number using Table 2 (see page 42).

Example If the consultation takes place at 9.35 am on 7 June 2004, this is how the lower trigram is calculated. Using Table 1, the numbers to add up would be 6 + 7 + 5 + 9 = 27, which corresponds to the time, day, month and year. The number 27 divided by 8 leaves a remainder of 3. Using Table 2, you will see this indicates the trigram Li.

If the consultation was made at 8 pm on the same day, the numbers to add would be 11 + 7 + 5 + 9 = 32, which is divisible by 8. So the number 8 is what indicates the lower trigram, in this case Kun.

Table 1: Numerical Aspects of the Hour, Day, Month and Year

Number	Hour	Month	Year
1	11 pm–1 am	February	1984, 1996
2	1 am–3 am	March	1985, 1997
3	3 am–5 am	April	1986, 1998
4	5 am–7 am	May	1987, 1999
5	7 am–9 am	June	1988, 2000
6	9 am–11 am	July	1989, 2001
7	11 am–1 pm	August	1990, 2002
8	1 pm–3 pm	September	1991, 2003
9	3 pm–5 pm	October	1992, 2004
10	5 pm–7 pm	November	1993, 2005
11	7 pm–9 pm	December	1994, 2006
12	9 pm–11 pm	January	1995, 2007

Table 2: Early Heaven Trigram Arrangement

Number	Trigram under Early Heaven Arrangement	Symbol	Number	Trigram under Early Heaven Arrangement	Symbol
1	Chien		5	Sun	
2	Tui		6	Kan	
3	Li		7	Ken	
4	Chen		8	Kun	

Table 3: Transforming Words into Numbers

1	2	3	4	5	6	7	8	9
A	B	C	D	E	F	G	H	I
J	K	L	M	N	O	P	Q	R
S	T	U	V	W	X	Y	Z	

Determining the Upper Trigram

The upper trigram is determined by making calculations based on the numerical aspect of the situation being investigated. This part of the oracle requires your intuitive judgment. To a large extent the accuracy of the advice generated by the I Ching will be determined by how well this upper trigram captures the essence of your question. So you need to be observant and aware of the symbolic relationship between the people and the objects involved, as well as any dimension of the question that catches your attention.

Essentially you will select from a broad range of the images, personalities and/or situations that you somehow, in your own mind, relate to the question you are asking the I Ching. At first, doing this might seem difficult, but over time you will realize just how observant you can be. When you start to look at the world in this knowing way, you will be both sharpening your powers of perception and allowing your inner mind to surface. Once you have decided on the person, object or image you wish to use to create your upper trigram, the next step is to assign it a numerical value.

This can be any of the following:

● the number of letters in a key word that describes the situation;

● the number of words in the question asked;

● the number of letters that make up the name of a significant person;

● the number of his/her telephone or address;

● a number associated with something that flashes through your mind as you contemplate the question (perhaps you recall a bird in flight or a dog running along the road, perhaps you hear a snippet of news on the radio or television that reminds you of something – see if a particular number stands out).

The most efficient way of transforming words into numbers is to go by the number equivalent of the letters of the alphabet, with 1 standing for A, 2 for B, 3 for C and so on. This is summarized in Table 3 (see page 42). The Chinese use the number of strokes that make up their Chinese word to arrive at a numerical representation.

As before, as soon as you have a number, reduce it to between 1 and 8 so that, by looking at Table 2, you can determine the equivalent upper trigram. Note, then, that the upper trigram is a numerical representation of your observations.

Example
If the name of the person requiring the consultation is Maria and you decide to use the numerical equivalent of her name, then the numbers to add up would be $4 + 1 + 9 + 9 + 1 = 24$. The trigram would be Kun, because 24 is divisible by 8.

With the lower and upper trigrams revealed, you now have the base hexagram and can start analysing it as described earlier. Look at the trigrams and study the attributes and the element relationships carefully, as these will provide immediate clues to the answers to your questions.

You will need to develop some proficiency in what you have learnt so far before going on to the next stage, which is to determine the changing line. Before you learn about the changing line, you should also study the additional information on the attributes of the trigrams (see pages 44–47) to help you analyse the hexagram you have created.

Attributes of the Trigrams

Trigram	Season	Direction	Weather
CHIEN	autumn	south under Early Heaven and north-west under Later Heaven arrangements	clear and bright; a beautiful day
CHEN	spring	north-east under Early Heaven and east under Later Heaven arrangements	thunder and lightning; loud
KAN	winter	west under Early Heaven and north under Later Heaven arrangements	heavy rain, showers, snow; gloomy
KEN	in between seasons	north-west under Early Heaven and north-east under Later Heaven arrangements	strengthens the other trigram indication

Partner indications	Travel	Location of lost object	Animal or symbol
tall, handsome or beautiful, long-limbed, firm sharp features, high forehead, good character	indicates you will be travelling within the next three months	can be found near a public building, in father's room, in a round container, on higher ground or near a metallic building	Ru yi (the instrument that symbolizes power), Kuan Kung (God of Wealth and God of War)
beautiful and classy but proud, with a tendency to arrogance; strong jaw, tendency to stubbornness	indicates travel by ship is beneficial	indicates object was lost outside the home or office in a place with trees, a park, forests, public highway or street; unlikely to be found	dragon
headstrong and jealous, curvy, tendency to plumpness, short, very materialistic and spendthrift, bad character	indicates loss or having something stolen	indicates object was lost somewhere in the north of the home, near water in a pond, a pool or in the drain; if lost outside the house unlikely to be found; blue container	tortoise, frog
clever, skilful, scholar, clean-cut, fair-skinned, graceful, sweet-natured and quiet, softly spoken, younger than you	beneficial to delay your travel	indicates object was lost somewhere in a corridor or passageway, near rocks, near mountains or concrete wall; square container	mountain, crystals

Attributes of the Trigrams

Trigram	Season	Direction	Weather
KUN	in between seasons	north under Early Heaven and south-west under Later Heaven arrangements	cloudy, dark and heavy rain, wet
LI	summer	east under Early Heaven and south under Later Heaven arrangements	sunshine, hot, drought, clear
SUN	spring	south-west under Early Heaven and south-east under Later Heaven arrangements	windy
TUI	autumn	south-east under Early Heaven and west under Later Heaven arrangements	cloudy, rain

Partner indications	Travel	Location of lost object	Animal or symbol
happy disposition and easygoing, motherly fussy type, oval face and sharp features, kind-hearted and warm, good conversationalist	beneficial to delay your travel	indicates object was lost somewhere in a basement or field; can be found inside a ceramic or glass container; look in the south-west	mare
hot-tempered, changeable, slim, dark-haired, difficult, fiery	beneficial to travel soon	indicates object was lost somewhere in the kitchen or fireplace, near window, empty room, beside or under a book	phoenix, birds, horse
tall and slim, but tendency to put on weight in later years; graceful and gentle; will bring you luck	beneficial to travel by land; do not fly	indicates object can be found inside a wooden container or in a rectangular room in the south-east of the house	plants
will bring you great happiness, charming personality, sweet, popular, dresses well, likely to be younger than you	a dispute could arise in your travels	indicates object can be found inside a metal container; could be lost in a lake or near a river bank	white tiger

Analysing the Trigrams

Study the attributes of the upper and lower trigrams based on this summary. You can see that the trigrams symbolize many things – directions, seasons, weather, members of a family, animals, symbols and so on. The summary here is not exhaustive and for those wanting a longer list I recommend that you invest in one of the original academic translations of the I Ching. This summary of the trigrams and their attributes can also be used to decipher the meanings of hexagrams derived under the Later Heaven arrangement.

You can also use the information here to help you derive the trigrams. For instance, if you are asking a question about your father you can use Chien as the upper trigram. Then see how this combines with the lower trigram formed by basing it on the exact time of the consultation. In the same way, if you are asking a question about your boyfriend you can use any of the three trigrams that indicate a man: Chen for someone aged between, say, 21 and 31; Ken for someone much younger and Kan for someone between the two. Which trigram you choose reflects your judgment. If you are unsure of yourself, you can always use the numerical equivalent of their name or a number they are especially fond of. Many people have their own 'lucky' numbers: for example, their date of birth, their address or a number that seems to feature a lot in their life.

Determining the Changing Line

After you have analysed the trigrams that make up the base hexagram, the next step is to determine the changing line.

The changing line refers to the line of the base hexagram that transforms the original hexagram into a new and predictive hexagram. The line itself offers a specific prediction related to the question asked and will either confirm your reading of the trigrams or introduce a new perspective for you to consider. It will create a new hexagram simply because the nature of the changing line is that it transforms lines from broken to solid or vice versa.

The way to determine the changing line under the Early Heaven arrangement is once again to use the four pillars of time – in other words, the hour, day, month and year of the consultation.

So, to repeat the example of a consultation taking place at 9.35 am on 7 June 2004 and using Table 1 again, the numbers to add up would be 6 + 7 + 5 + 9 = 27. However, to find the changing line, the key number is 6 rather than 8. If the total is 6 or less, that is the number of the changing line, counting from the bottom up. If it is more, you divide the total by 6 and use the remainder. In this example, the changing line is 3 (27 divided by 6 is 4 with a remainder of 3): that is, the third line from the bottom. For the meanings of these lines, see Chapter 5.

Determining the New Predictive Hexagram

With the changing line you will be able to determine the new predictive hexagram. This is done simply by transforming the changing line to its opposite. So, if the changing line is solid it becomes broken and if it is broken it becomes solid.

Example
Here is how the hexagram Chien is changed to the hexagram Kuai when the changing line is the sixth – that is, the top – line. Once you have the base hexagram, the changing line and the new predictive hexagram determined, you are ready to go deeper in your analysis. So far, you have studied only the trigrams, but now you can look at the whole hexagram. You have two to consider and it is the second, predictive hexagram that contains the prophetic aspect associated with your question.

The base hexagram allows you to analyse the trigrams and obtain an initial reading and description of the situation. The changing line and predictive hexagram are for you to read and reflect over, using the meanings indicated in Chapter 5 when you consult the texts of the I Ching.

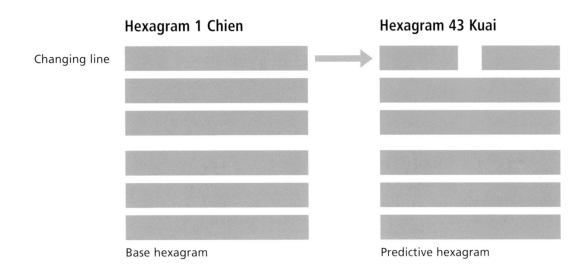

Hexagram 1 Chien

Hexagram 43 Kuai

Changing line

Base hexagram

Predictive hexagram

Later Heaven Trigram Arrangement Method

This is a more advanced method of the Plum Blossom Oracle. It places greater emphasis on your powers of observation and intuitive judgments, because both the upper and lower trigrams that make up the base hexagram are derived directly from observed phenomena.

It is not usually advisable to use this method until you have become really proficient in consulting the I Ching as an oracle and have developed genuine confidence in your ability to pick out something you instinctively feel offers a significant reading of the situation. However, when you have reached this stage, the Later Heaven method is the one that enables you to communicate directly with your inner mind and your own wisdom consciousness.

Each of the trigrams in the Later Heaven arrangement has an assigned number that differs from those in the Early Heaven arrangement, although the way to obtain the number for an observed situation, image or object is the same.

Because of the importance of observed phenomena, you will need to encourage a state of mind that allows you to develop your powers of observation as acutely as possible, heightening your visual and aural senses. To get the most out of the oracle, it is also necessary to develop your sensitivity to moods, ambience and the attitudes of people around you. All these observations can be factored into the identification of the trigram.

Using this method, you must also become thoroughly familiar with the structure and texts of the I Ching, as great importance is attached to these as well as to the element interactions of the trigrams.

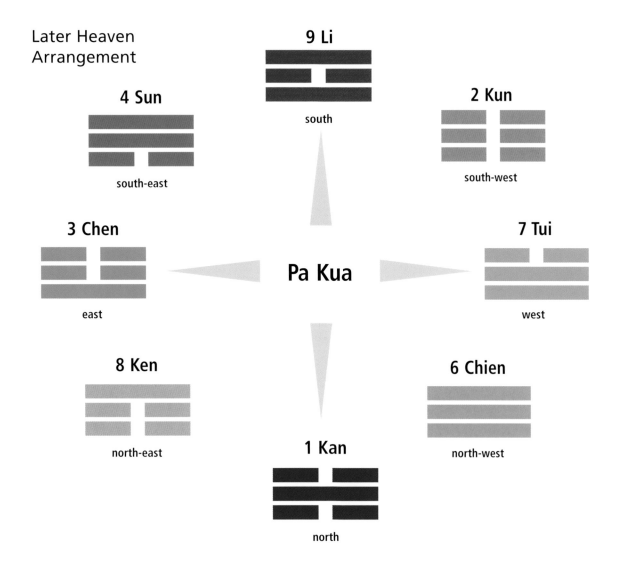

Later Heaven Arrangement

9 Li
south

4 Sun
south-east

2 Kun
south-west

3 Chen
east

Pa Kua

7 Tui
west

8 Ken
north-east

1 Kan
north

6 Chien
north-west

Determining Both Upper and Lower Trigrams

Since the upper and lower trigrams of the base hexagram are derived directly from the situation itself, follow the same procedure in both cases. Note that this method relies heavily on your judgment.

You will need to observe and select two aspects of the situation, event, person or question about which you are consulting the oracle. This can be related to colours, moods, clothes, sounds or places – just about anything that catches your attention and can be transformed into a numerical aspect, either by converting the letters of key words into numbers (using Table 3 on page 52) or by identifying a numerical dimension.

If you are consulting the I Ching about an interview for a new job, you could use the name of the company for one aspect, while the other could relate to something you see that you feel is somehow relevant.

Example If you wore a white suit to an interview, you could use the words 'wearing white suit' to create a trigram. Using Table 3, add up the numbers as shown below.

Wearing will be 5 + 5 + 1 + 9 + 9 + 5 + 7 = 41
White will be 5 + 8 + 9 + 2 + 5 = 29
Suit will be 1 + 3 + 9 + 2 = 15
So 41 + 29 + 15 = 85 and 85 divided by 8 is 10 remainder 5. (See pages 40–43 for a full explanation.)

The trigram generated by number 5 will be Kun if the subject is a woman and Ken if the subject is a man (see Table 2). This is because the number 5 becomes 2 if the subject is a woman and 8 if the subject is a man.

Next decide which of the two aspects best describes the subject of your question. In this case, the subject aspect will be the trigram Kun if the questioner is a woman and Ken if the questioner is a man.

Table 2: Later Heaven Trigram Arrangement

Number	Trigram under Later Heaven Arrangement	Symbol	Number	Trigram under Later Heaven Arrangement	Symbol
1	Kan		5	Ken (for men)	
2	Kun		6	Chien	
3	Chen		7	Tui	
4	Sun		8	Ken	
5	Kun (for women)		9	Li	

Table 3: Transforming Words into Numbers

1	2	3	4	5	6	7	8	9
A	B	C	D	E	F	G	H	I
J	K	L	M	N	O	P	Q	R
S	T	U	V	W	X	Y	Z	

The subject aspect becomes the upper trigram.

The other aspect then becomes the fate aspect and this becomes the lower trigram. For example, if a song on the radio about three little boys caught your attention then the trigram for the fate aspect could be generated by the number 3.

To summarize:

- Obtain numerical equivalents of two aspects of the situation under question.

- Designate one the subject aspect; this will become the upper trigram.

- Designate the other the fate aspect; this will become the lower trigram.

- Determine the trigram(s) in accordance with Table 2, which indicates the trigram that matches the number you have derived from the observed situation based on the Later Heaven arrangement of the trigrams (remember, this is different from the Early Heaven arrangement).

As in the first method, once you have the lower and upper trigrams you can combine them to create the base hexagram (see page 49). Identify this hexagram before moving on to work out the changing line, which will then give you the predictive outcome as well as the new predictive hexagram.

Determining the Changing Line

Under this method the changing line is determined by adding the numbers of the upper and lower trigrams (see Table 2). For this example, the upper trigram is Ken and the lower trigram is Chen. Using Table 2, the numbers to add up would be 8 + 3 = 11. To find the changing line, the key number is 6. If the total is 6 or less, that will be the number of the changing line. If the total exceeds 6, divide it by 6 and the remainder will give you the number of the changing line (remember to count from the bottom up). In this example, the changing line is 5 (11 divided by 6 is 1 with a remainder of 5): that is, the fifth line from the bottom. Once you have the changing line you will be able to get the new hexagram, which will give you a sense of the ultimate outcome of the situation.

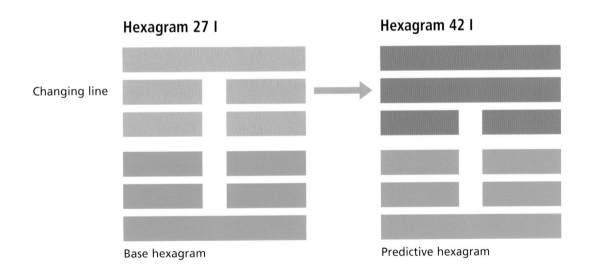

Hexagram 27 I

Changing line

Base hexagram

Hexagram 42 I

Predictive hexagram

CHAPTER 3
Predictions of the 64 Hexagrams

The I Ching is an amazing energy force, which becomes stimulated as soon as questions are addressed to it. As an oracle the I Ching cuts into the heart of any given situation and offers advice by predicting a possible outcome or describing a developing scenario. Communicating with the I Ching requires speaking to it in its own language – through the symbols of its 64 hexagrams.

The Chien Hexagrams

 Chien

The power of heaven is infinite and long-lasting

Good fortune is coming your way

Every dispute can be harmoniously resolved

You will find a cure for your illness

The operations of your company proceed smoothly

There is happiness and harmony ahead

 Hsu

The image of a dragon with its pearl brings success

Brilliant awakening is coming to you – good news

The marriage you want will take place

Your business enterprise will make good profits

Happiness is coming

All committed projects are successful

If you persevere there is no blame

 Ta Chuang

The power of the great brings abundance

You have good materials to work with

This is a fortunate time when everything is blessed
    with success

You can continue with confidence and courage

Travel will bring many benefits

Disputes are favourably resolved

Meetings with friends go smoothly

You will find a cure for your sickness

 Ta Ch'u

The taming of the great clarifies everything

Your business travel will yield good results

There is good news coming through the mail

New friendships bring opportunities

Clarity emerges where there was confusion

The man proposes and the girl accepts

Unhappiness is soon transformed into happiness

You have the capability to rise to the challenge

Tai

Three times good news comes to you

There is continuous good fortune

Peace and harmony prevail in your environment

Business and travel luck favour you

Troubles and disputes find a quick solution

Associates are agreeable to your plans

Relationships enjoy a period of great harmony

Someone you have not seen for a long time
    reappears

There are good indications of a forthcoming
    marriage

Ta Yu

You have possessions in great measure – be happy

When the sentiment of people is negative, do
    not act

Your success and wealth do not create problems

What you have lost will be returned to you

You can locate a partner with no difficulty

Marriage plans can proceed with no problems

If you want recognition, you will get it

If you apply for a job you will be successful

You will meet someone important in the next
    30 days

Hsiao Ch'u

Taming the small suggests a need for patience

This is a time best spent watching and consolidating

Going to see the great man brings little benefits

Crossing the great waters does you little good

Relationships are in a state of suspension

Business travels do not yield any new business

Not a good time to expand

This is a good time to relax and go on a retreat

Kuai

Determination gets you everywhere, reaps you
    benefits

There is a new baby coming into your household

Your prosperity luck has arrived – be prepared …

A legal complication is favourably and amicably
    settled

Sickness is completely cured – medicines will work

Your business problems will be resolved to your
    satisfaction

You will have success in your examinations

Your job application will open new opportunities

The Chen Hexagrams

Wu Wang

The image of birds in captivity suggests a trap

Be careful of becoming embroiled in a negative
situation

Do not be overly trusting as you could get trapped

There are gossip and troubles if you proceed

Your plans and commitments look dangerous – try
to withdraw

You have missed the boat – wait for a more
propitious time

Your lover is betraying you – be careful

Your health is taking a turn for the worse

Chun

The image of an ill wind that blows no good

There is chaos at the start – plan carefully

Entanglements cause you to have a frustrating time

Sickness does not find immediate relief

Quarrels and disputes get worse before they get
better

There is grave danger of gossip getting out of hand

Fair-weather friends disappoint you – but you must
not react

Jealous business rivals mount a verbal assault on you

This is a trying time – go on holiday!

Chen

The image of thunder brings good news

Your fame spreads like the sounds of the golden bell

You will attract recognition from all directions

You will enjoy excellent money and wealth luck

You will have a very good business partner

Influential friends help and protect you

Job applications meet with success easily

You will receive a high appointment

What is lost is brought back to you

I

The image of nourishment is most auspicious

Even the king stops by your home – great honour

All your plans find favour with the authorities

Sickness and problems find cures and solutions

There is an excellent person helping you – a mentor

This period brings the promise of a rise in rank

There is good fortune coming to you in the next
three months

Hostilities evaporate and misunderstandings are
cleared up

Fu

The symbol of earth above wood brings bad news
Harmony flies out of the window as people become
    hostile
Even a friend becomes an enemy
This is a bad time to see the great man
You need patience to endure this time of confusion
When things are uncertain it is best to retreat
There is no useful information coming to you

I

The winter plum blossom bursts into bloom
You experience a sudden spurt of good energy
Misfortunes transform into good fortune
Your legal problems are harmoniously sorted out
Travel brings benefits personally and professionally
What has been missing is now found
After a period of trying times good fortune comes
Your plans can be revived

Shih Ho

A starving beggar receives his first meal in days
Hard times seem to have come to an end
You will find pleasure in wining and dining
There will be a joyous double-happiness celebration
In legal tussles you will come out winning
Everything now favours you and you can proceed
For those who are single, there is romance in store
Travels are beneficial – the further the better
The agony of loneliness finds respite

Sui

The road ahead of you looks paved with gold
Your plans proceed with few difficulties
Sickness and gossip have no place in your life
This is a time that favours you
A new commitment brings great happiness
There is the possibility of a new family member
Employees bring you good fortune
What is lost can be found
Marriage is a possibility

The Kan Hexagrams

 Sung

The image is of conflict and hostility

There are indications that you are wasting your time and money

Marriage partners cause distress

Business partners create misfortunes

New commitments will not bring you happiness

There is a shortage of money

There are obstacles that block everything you do

 Kan

The image of the Abysmal is like seeing a mirage

Reflections of glory have little substance

You find it difficult to differentiate between real and fake gold

You have no luck in getting recognition

Your hopes for a marriage proposal are dashed

Business partnerships have no foundation

Sickness finds no cure

What you have lost is lost for ever

 Hsieh

The symbol suggests birds flying out of their cages

There is a release from serious entanglements

Money problems become less taxing

Help arrives from good friends

Sickness will see a marked improvement

Your social life takes off – suddenly you are very popular

Your project finds backers

There is a new assignment or job possibility this month

 Meng

The image of youthful foolishness

It seems you are wasting your time and effort

Your social life is riddled with idle gossip

You will face serious setbacks in your travels

There is a need for great caution

Be prepared for a shortage of money

You have to endure a loss of wealth

Your income will be reduced – be prudent

Shih

Dried leaves wither in the period of drought

There is help after a bad time

A period of hard work and frustration ends

Worries and problems are transformed into
	happiness

There is a good harvest for all your efforts

Plans find a favourable response

At work things begin to look up for you

There is good news coming to you

Everything becomes easier

 Wei Chi

The prediction is one of sadness

Misfortunes bring a time of tears and sorrow

Business travels cause much distress – better to
	postpone

Avoid disputes for they will bring you more troubles

Do not engage in hostilities because you will lose

Marriage plans go awry – better to wait

The period of misfortune lasts for 28 days

If you are patient, misfortunes will transform into
	good fortune

 Huan

The image of separation brings frustration

Your marriage plans meet with failure

There is no marriage proposal

There is a great divide between you and success

Joint ventures simply do not succeed

There are many obstacles facing you

There is no merit in dreaming empty dreams

This is not a good time to start new ventures

 K'un

The image is one of being cheated by friends

All your plans and projects do not find favour

Beware of fair-weather friends – they can cause
	much distress

If you are careful in whom to trust you will avoid
	misfortunes

Better to seek out the company of true friends

Do not desert your old friends for new friends

Your job application cannot succeed

If you are sick this is not a time when you can
	get better

Beware of sweet-talking salesmen

The Ken Hexagrams

Tun

The image of the sun being covered by dark clouds

This is a time to stay at home, not travel

Inviting people into your home brings good fortune

Take a conciliatory approach and compromise

Arrogance and anger lead to serious misfortunes

Publicity at this time attracts bad luck – stay
 low-key

New endeavours meet with obstacles – postpone
 plans

Not a good time for marriage

Do not invest time or money in anything new

Hsiao Kuo

If you act with firmness there is success

Prevarication will only cause you to attract
 misfortune

You do not need to be perfect to succeed

It is foolish not to carry out a good idea

In life there are times to be bold – this is the time

Do not allow others to discourage you

If you speak up now your relationships will make
 progress

Search hard enough and you will find what you seek

Remember, faint heart never won fair lady!

Chien

Danger and obstructions are predicted

The more you move forward the harder it will be

A time to cut your losses and retreat

This is a time when patience and toughness are vital

Marriage goes through a rough patch

Relationships simply cannot succeed

Travelling brings empty returns

Be extra wary of dangers ahead

Ken

Your ideas are simply too impractical to work

You must ignore frivolous gossip and form your
 own opinions

This is a time when inaction is the best course
 to follow

Business plans cannot take off

You need to go back to the drawing board

Think through your aspirations before you act

It is a good idea to be cautious

Not a good time to travel

Ch'ien

Good fortune falls from out of the sky

If you are working hard you will discover gold

There is success for those not expecting it

Your new project will find instant success – be
encouraged

Marriage plans move forward easily and without
obstruction

Business moves aggressively forward

Influential help comes from important people

 Lu

The image of falling trees and burning forests

Nothing benefits if you get this hexagram

There is no merit at all in your plan – drop
the project

Travelling brings no material rewards

This is a good time to retreat and meditate

Accept defeat with honour and good grace

The superior man bows low – no blame

A good time to take a break from work

 Chien

The red bird flies to the western hills

Unexpected opportunity comes from an unlikely
source

Prosperity and recognition are coming for you

Travelling to another country is beneficial

The medicine and cures work well – you will soon
feel better

Misunderstandings evaporate and in their place
is goodwill

Employees support you wholeheartedly

You will find favour with financiers – proceed
with confidence

Slow and steady wins the race – no need to rush

 Hsien

A beautiful woman cannot be won in an instant

If you take your time you will succeed

Despite things looking unexciting there is gold
hidden within

The superior man bides his time and has good
fortune

Taking your medicine faithfully brings recovery

An old love comes back into your life – it is
auspicious

Dig deeper and you will discover new opportunities

The Kun Hexagrams

P'i

The dragon is captured – progress comes to an instant halt

Ideas and actions are useless in the face of bad luck

Success is hard to come by – better to wait

Your love life is stagnating – best to go with the flow

When things come to a standstill look within for solutions

Delays will cause you to lose money – but what is to be done?

Sickness will cause you to have a setback

Pi

The dragon boat is loaded with gold ingots

An auspicious wind blows good fortune into your home

There is plenty of goodwill and rejoicing

Legal problems are resolved

Money owed to you is recovered

Marriage plans proceed smoothly

A double-happiness *hei see* occasion (such as a marriage or a baby's christening) takes place

Longevity, birthdays, a new baby, a marriage – all are possible

Yu

The dragon is released – he flies high into the skies

Happiness comes from continuous good fortune

Business meets with huge success

Love relationships can lead to marriage

Gossip and slander evaporate into the air

Mentors and influential benefactors bring new business

Your marriage misunderstandings get resolved amicably

Children bring honour and happiness to parents

Po

The dry land gets rainfall and flowers bloom

An important introduction brings you cause for celebration

Journeys prove interesting and exciting

Your job applications are all successful

Legal entanglements will be resolved

Sicknesses find good cures

Misunderstandings are cleared up

K'un

Hunger is appeased and the belly is full

A happy time when mothers give a helping hand

You will receive the promotion you want

Bad news turns out to be frivolous – and no cause
for alarm

Troubles and problems are solved with little
difficulty

You succeed in getting an appointment with an
important person

Favours women – there is good news coming

 Kuan

Cranes and magpies make for unlikely pals

Within the household there is no harmony

The living situation is cold and unfriendly –
move out

At the office there is no communication

It is advisable to observe without comments

Plans for new ventures find no takers

In the midst of unhappiness there is one
bright spark

Expected guests and letters do not show up

 Chin

There is gold in your garden if only you know it

You do not expect it but wealth comes to you
suddenly

Clouds that hide the bright and glorious sun soon
blow over

Wait for a positive sign before acting – it will
soon appear

Action should happen only when the time is
auspicious

When you clean your house you may find a
forgotten treasure

Family attics can hold hidden wish-fulfilling gems

 Ts'ui

Crossing the dragon gate brings a promotion

The fish is transformed into a dragon – upward
mobility

Despite many setbacks you achieve your goal

Months of hard work will soon find recognition

Honours and prosperity come to you easily now

The prize is won – it is a time of celebration

New opportunities open new ways to wealth

Those hostile to you before are now your supporters

In politics, enemies lose their teeth

The Sun Hexagrams

Kou

Long-lost friends meet unexpectedly and find gold

Everything moves along smoothly for you – no obstacles

It benefits you to cross the great waters

Travel brings huge and unexpected benefits

Wealth luck coming to you will last a long time

You have the karma to attain high rank and great honour

Your family enjoys the fruits of your advancement

Dangers that previously threatened the patriarch are now resolved

Ching

An old well suddenly fills with spring water

After a period of tough times you encounter good fortune

You enjoy increasing popularity and praise

Misfortunes have left you – all your plans succeed

Money comes to you from many different sources

Abroad or at home you enjoy good fortune

Marriage luck is at an all-time high – take advantage

This is a good time to improve your house Feng Shui

Everything you do has a good chance to succeed

Heng

A good harvest comes at a most auspicious time

Business luck is encouraging you to be an entrepreneur

A marriage proposal meets with a favourable response

Travel luck is good – the longer the journey the better

A period of ill health is now over

Gossip against you has no chance to hurt you

There is total release from legal entanglements

Misunderstandings are cleared up amicably

Friends support you – it is a happy time

Ku

To improve your situation you need to consider carefully

If you act with honour and integrity you will reap rewards

Misfortune is experienced when you act dishonestly

Travelling for business is a total waste of time

No need for tension – what is meant to happen will happen

Whatever you have lost cannot be recovered

If you are philosophical about loss you will feel better

Slow and steady progress is preferable to being in a hurry

Sheng

Good fortune comes like the first blooms of spring

There is excellent expansion and growth luck

Communication from around the globe brings
good news

The sun shines brightly and benevolently on all
your plans

Projects move ahead with no major obstructions

You can attain the level of recognition you want

It benefits you to meet the great man

Your family benefits from your extreme good
fortune

Sun

The wind moves the boat along – there is smooth
sailing

Wind and water bring you extreme good fortune

Marriage plans proceed without a hitch

Business arrangements with partners go smoothly

All your financial expectations are exceeded

Sales improvements lift you to a higher league

You will gain popularity and a great name

Ting

The cauldron creates a fresh new brew – good
fortune

You will receive word of money coming to you

There is prosperity for all members of your family

Travel is most beneficial at this time

You will find a marriage partner very soon

Legal threats evaporate and everything is settled
favourably

Sickness is cured – the medicines work efficiently

Ta Kuo

As long as you can see the peak, keep walking

Living in a dream world can be harmful – you must
be realistic

You encounter difficulties at work and in business

You need to have patience and to develop yourself

This is not the time to be arrogant or ambitious

Everything you try to do meets with failure

This is a very frustrating time – try to be
philosophical

In life there are highs and lows – this is the low
period

The Li Hexagrams

T'ung Jen

When the family has harmony heaven smiles on you

Wherever you wish to move to you will have good fortune

Partnerships expand as good fortune brings happiness

Marriages are favoured – promise of long-lasting happiness

Love relationships will have a happy ending

Any new commitments will be a mistake

Old friends support you while new friends stay indifferent

Feng

The repolished mirror shines like the full moon

Love and romance enjoy favourable outcomes

Suddenly you see everything clearly

Bad luck gives way to an auspicious period of abundance

You will benefit from travel and long-distance communication

All business deals will bring extra benefits

Marriage problems are resolved harmoniously

Sickness finds a suitable cure

Chi Chi

Your name is placed up high on the golden plaque

If you retire now you will go in a blaze of glory

You are blessed with many grateful friends and supporters

Your descendants will benefit from your good name

Whatever you may have lost in the past is now recovered

An old adversary greets you with genuine respect

You will know the true meaning of friendship very soon

You are looking ahead to a prosperous and meaningful period

Pi

Love blooms – the blushing young lady finds her young beau

Thoughts of marriage bring you a most suitable match

This hexagram symbolizes a truly happy wedding party

Happiness comes after months of misunderstandings

Travelling benefits your luck and your career

Whatever you may have lost is now found again

Your life moves smoothly along a prosperous road

Ming I

A darkening of the light closes out the sun

Misfortune strikes with ungraceful haste

You should stay inactive but alert

Friends turn against you and supporters desert you

These are troubled times – watch out

There is no good news on the horizon – use caution

Disorder creates chaos, which in turn brings
misfortune

It is hard to build bridges at this time – try at a
better time

Chia Jen

Your reflection looks beautiful, but it is still a
reflection

You are going through a slow period – things will
pick up

If you cannot do anything about your situation,
worrying cannot help

Business partnerships could be heading for a
breakdown

Irreconcilable marriage differences lead to heartbreak

What has been taken from you will be returned

Fame, recognition, long-term success – all are hard
to come by

New commitments lead to suffering

Li

The sun's light brightens even the dullest moods

There is continuous good fortune from heaven

All sadness, problems and sickness will evaporate
quickly

Everything succeeds because this time favours your
endeavours – be bold

There is every reason to be confident

If you get this be encouraged – success awaits you

Ko

Time for a major upheaval in your life

With rain falling there is water to make your
garden grow

All your best-laid plans move along with great
energy

There will be an excellent harvest this time

Caution is a good word to guard against arrogance

Travelling brings many new opportunities, especially
to relocate

A message from an old friend deserves your serious
attention

What was previously lost is easily found

The Tui Hexagrams

Lu

Birds droop their heads in the shade

There will be a period of inactivity

This is a time to prolong negotiation if you want
benefits

Travel is advisable – there will be new avenues to
investigate

A good time to focus on your studies

If you are well prepared the sky is the limit

When you have mastered the skills money will
be plentiful

Kuei Mei

The marrying girl brings misfortunes

Attempting the impossible can only lead to disaster

Despite great effort there is no achievement

Your time has not yet come – so nothing benefits

This is not the time to do anything – no blame

Contemplating marriage at this time is a mistake

The suitor is insincere – it is better to be more
patient

Career goals are hard to bring to fruition

Cheih

Getting the help of the great man, your problems
evaporate

Troubles disappear when the great man arrives

There will be no more legal entanglements

Great success and fame can be achieved – but be
humble

When one has good fortune the sky is the limit

Your career takes off when you catch the eye of the
big boss

There is useful information coming to you – use it
carefully

Be diplomatic with older people when you succeed

Sun

The cart has lost its wheel – how can it move?

Misfortune comes in the form of strong opposition

Arrogance is what has brought you misfortune

When one knows humility one attracts good fortune

Help comes to those who are not too proud to ask

At this stage of your life you can be too ignorant

Experience is often the best teacher

If you learn from your mistakes then any loss is
worthwhile

Lin

Compassion attracts a special kind of good fortune

Commitments are easy to fulfil – no need to worry

Do not make promises too easily – think first

Getting married will bring you good fortune

The new job sounds very promising indeed – take it

Problems with the boss were in your mind only

You will gain an unexpected promotion

Family members are especially helpful this month

Chung Fu

More a time for deep contemplation than action

This is a time when inner truths will surface

Money luck is elusive – better to wait

Sickness can be cured – but it takes a long time

If your business goes through a tough time hang
in there

Work situations are tense – stay calm

At home inner tensions cause feelings of insecurity

Love relationships turn cool – respect each other's
space

Kuei

You have incurred the displeasure of someone
powerful

Only time can lessen the venom being directed
at you

This is a time when you are walking on thin ice

You can only avoid disaster if you act and react
carefully

Be cautious when you travel – there are hidden
dangers

If you are at school or college you can expect a
disappointment

Do not walk in haste – take one step at a time

Tui

Like going to the God realms

An extremely happy prediction that foretells great
success

There are many excellent opportunities coming

You can attain your heart's desire with little effort

There is no gossip or slander that can stick to you

Plans and projects find willing takers – be bold

This is a marvellous prediction and whatever is in
your mind you will achieve

A time for celebration and great joyousness

CHAPTER 4
Asking Questions and Interpreting Answers

When you use the *Plum Blossom Oracle* regularly you will
find yourself making a conscious effort to observe and
recall things you see and words you hear. In no time you
will find this becomes second nature and your senses will
be immeasurably heightened. You will begin to live in a
state of greater awareness, which will bring benefits that
go far beyond being able to read the oracle. The next stage
is to maximize your use of the *I Ching* by sharpening your
understanding of its answers.

Interpreting the Hexagrams

Interpreting the hexagrams is usually fairly straightforward. Mostly the I Ching advises on timing, but it also points the way to other options and draws attention to things you should consider when making choices. You can then pursue matters with further questions. You will need to get used to having a dialogue with the I Ching, so choose part of the day when you have plenty of time and can ask your questions in an unhurried way.

If, however, you are looking for a straight Yes/No reply I suggest you use the Early Heaven arrangement method, and supplement your element analyses by reading Chapter 4. Whether you use this or Chapter 5, which contains descriptions of the six lines of each hexagram, it is worth familiarizing yourself thoroughly with the hexagrams themselves. When you have constructed the base and predictive hexagrams and taken note of the changing line, the next step is interpretation. As we have already seen, you start by examining the trigrams that make up the hexagram, as it is vital to know what they are telling you before moving on. You will need to study the element interactions of both sets of trigrams, primary and nuclear.

To recap, the primary trigrams are the external trigrams of any hexagram, symbolizing the obvious and easily detected forces at work in the prevailing situation. They also reveal the environmental factors affecting the outcome of the question. They reveal who the main players are, what the weather will be like, what season is significant to the question, what information there is about travel, illness, food and so on. To get a feel for what the trigrams are saying, take a look at the chart of attributes assigned to each of the trigrams on pages 44–7. This will indicate whether the preliminary reading is positive or negative and whether it holds out the promise of a beneficial or harmful outcome.

Note that when analysing the trigrams, the lower or upper trigram of both the primary and nuclear trigram can be referring to the person asking the question. This depends on the trigram itself.

The nuclear trigrams reveal hidden motives and ambitions. They are a more accurate indication of the underlying forces and tensions that may be clouding the situation. They indicate the presence of hidden friends and secret enemies and provide information on other less obvious aspects.

Analysing the Elements

To obtain a preliminary reading of the two sets of trigrams, first identify the elements and other attributes of each of the four trigrams. See if you can detect a pattern. Allow your intuition to flow into the reading. Be guided by the way the elements of the upper and lower trigrams are interacting, as this is an excellent guide to how the situation is likely to unfold. Use the productive, exhaustive and destructive cycles (see pages 36–8) of the elements to help you determine the positive and negative possibilities of the outcome.

In the Plum Blossom Oracle both earth and earth, and water and water, always indicate good fortune. The hexagrams Kan (water doubled), Ken (mountain doubled) and K'un (earth doubled) also indicate the promise of good fortune. However, Li (fire doubled)

is usually dangerous and Chien and Tui (metal doubled) can often cause endless problems. The elements of wood and metal, and water with fire are likewise damaging, indicating discord between friends. Remember, though, that some of the trigrams can stand for two elements: for example, Tui stands for metal but also has the attributes of a lake, so it is water too. Meanwhile, water and fire, though destructive, can also be extremely auspicious, as when fire turns water into steam energy.

Consulting the Texts

Once you have finished analysing the element relationships you can proceed to the texts of the hexagrams and the changing lines, which reveal more information on the luck associated with each hexagram. They will give you a broader perspective and often lead you into conversation with the I Ching.

You can also go beyond the texts by interpreting the imagery implicit in the trigrams and their effects on each other, both primary and nuclear. When you approach the I Ching in this way, it becomes clear that the possibilities for interpretation are vast, and once you factor in the impact of observed phenomena as additional signals from the cosmos, the true power of the I Ching as an oracle is revealed.

The symbols of the trigrams are best analysed in association with the texts of the hexagrams, as they will combine to tell you a story. Usually they reveal something that is not immediately obvious. Sometimes more than one message is given. Also the I Ching tends to presents short- and long-term solutions to the issues engaging your mind. In some cases a time-frame is made clear. It is from the range of information given by the hexagram that an experienced consultant can see what is being advised.

Learning to Ask the Right Questions

When consulting the I Ching, it is helpful to be very clear in your mind about what you really want to know. You must be focused, serious and calm. If you are agitated, the mood is sure to spill over into the reading. Meditate on the matter for a while before proceeding with any consultation. It is a good idea to write down your question in a notebook, as this improves concentration. Phrase your question as accurately as possible.

Read through the texts of the hexagrams to get a feel for how the I Ching speaks, after which communication will be much easier. When you are familiar with the kind of answers the I Ching gives, you will know how to tailor your questions to get a more focused reply.

Sample Questions to Ask the Oracle

BUSINESS

1   Should I invest [give the amount] in this new venture?
2   Should I go into partnership with [give the name]?
3   If I expand now will my new shop be successful?
4   Will my application for a bank loan succeed?
5   Will my diversification plans succeed?
6   Can my sales/profits improve this year?
7   Will I win the contract [describe it] I am after?
8   Should I consult [give the name] about this matter?
9   Will my expansion overseas into [give the name] succeed?
10 Should I acquire this company [give the name] for [give the amount]?

CAREER

1 Should I accept this new assignment [describe it]?

2 Will I secure this promotion to become manager?

3 Is this transfer to [give the name] good for my long-term career?

4 Should I accept this relocation to [give the name]?

5 Will I get a pay rise this year?

6 Can I be made a director of the company?

7 Will it benefit me to resign from my present job now?

8 Is this a good time to have a chat with my boss?

9 Should I volunteer to take on this assignment [give the name]?

10 Should I sack this employee [give the name]?

FAMILY

1 Can my marriage problems be resolved?

2 I want to divorce my wife/husband – is this a good move?

3 I want to break off this affair – will I be successful?

4 Should we move near to our in-laws?

5 Should I confide my true feelings to him/her?

6 Will my son do well in his exams?

7 Can my mother recover from her illness?

8 Will my husband succeed in his plans?

9 Should I adopt this baby?

10 Should I let my child go overseas to study?

LOVE LIFE

1 Does he/she really love me?

2 Is there a long-term future to our relationship?

3 Will he/she go out with me if I ask directly?

4 Should I marry him/her?

5 Will he/she make a good husband/wife in the long term?

6 Will this man be able to provide for me in marriage?

7 Will this man stay faithful?

8 Does he/she love me more than [give the name]?

9 Will he ask me to marry him this year?

10 If I ask her, will she agree to marry me?

STUDIES

1 Will I get all the results I expect?

2 Should I give up this particular course [give the name]?

3 Should I consider changing schools?

4 Will I be successful if I change course?

5 If I go to university will my job prospects improve?

6 Will I get a scholarship to go to university?

7 Will my plans to study abroad succeed?

8 Will I be admitted to the university I want [give the name]?

9 Will I succeed in getting the first-class honours I am expecting?

10 Should I consider postgraduate work?

Interpreting the Answers

Never forget that the predictive hexagram will reveal a specific answer to a specific question. If you obtain a seemingly negative answer, do not worry. It refers only to the question asked and should not be taken to apply to your general situation. There is usually only one answer to each question at that moment. I always phrase my question carefully and then reflect on the single sentence in the answer that appeals instantly to my senses. Often that sparks something within me, and I have solved many puzzling questions this way.

You will discover that the key to success in consulting the I Ching lies in meditative reflection on the answers given. So practise sitting back and reflecting on your question in what I call 'analytical meditation'. Ask yourself a silent 'Why?' And when you deem it absolutely necessary, ask the I Ching a second question that builds on the first, and so on. One question leads to an answer, which then leads to the next question.

You will find this interactive approach more satisfying than a straightforward question and answer session. In time you will gain a certain familiarity with the hexagrams and the accompanying lines, but even then you will still be amazed by the I Ching's versatility and the relevance of its responses.

You know that you must always look at the symbolic relationships between the lines of the trigrams contained in any hexagram and study the relationship of the trigrams with each other. Usually insights will come to you as you reflect deeply on the meanings of the lines, especially the changing lines.

In the Plum Blossom Oracle there will be a single changing line. Consider the text of the changing line carefully. It usually offers a straightforward good or bad fortune response, but sometimes it will open your mind to other options. It can also ask you about what you witnessed on the particular day of the consultation. Changing lines always indicate some kind of development, so you react and respond to what is being advised.

The Changing Line

Note that when there are changing lines, two hexagrams are indicated. The first describes your present situation and the second hexagram contains the predicted outcome. This can often be contradictory and even seem meaningless. Study the outer and hidden trigrams of both hexagrams. Reflect on them and engage your mind seriously. The meaning and prediction will be both obvious and obscure, so refrain from jumping to conclusions. When challenged this way, it is a good idea to seek further clarification from the I Ching.

The Language of the I Ching

It takes time to become familiar with the language of the I Ching, but this is the only way to learn how to interpret the predictions given. Once you have studied how events and outcomes are described and advice is offered, you will come to see that the I Ching is a gentle communicator, rarely putting excessive emphasis on any advice. This reflects its basic philosophy, which is to adopt a detached view of all situations. It gives advice with a dispassionate air, judging all situations to contain the seeds of both good and bad fortune.

The I Ching considers that everything is in a constant state of flux. It also assumes that everyone has the power and capacity to change the outcome of situations. Thus the texts are usually worded as pieces of specific advice shrouded in colourful language. When you consult the I Ching about a certain course of action, it often responds with a cryptic answer. Here are three common responses and an analysis of what they might mean. Once you understand the way these phrases are interpreted, their usefulness will become clear.

It benefits to cross the great water. This might mean exactly what it says: that is, it will be beneficial to make a journey, take a trip or agree to a holiday. But it can also mean that a risk is worth taking, or something that appears difficult to undertake will be beneficial in the long run. As the person asking the question, you will have to look beyond the words and relate the answer to the situation facing you.

The honourable man ... Here the I Ching refers to the accepted moral code of behaviour followed by the Taoists. In the past in China great store was set on behaving in a polite 'correct' way. Moreover, it was important for scholars and the educated classes to behave well and set an example. There is a moral consciousness underlying many of the I Ching's texts, so an honourable man is one who follows the correct course of action.

It furthers one to see the great man. Here the I Ching is advising you to pluck up your courage and put forward your proposal. The indications are that you will in all likelihood meet with a favourable response. Seeing the 'great man' here refers to the boss, the leader or someone who can be your mentor.

No blame ... This is a common phrase with which any student of I Ching will become familiar. It suggests that life's outcomes should not result in the apportioning of blame. The I Ching recognizes that situations are often beyond your control. You can try hard to follow a course of action and yet the outcome may not be beneficial for everyone. As long as your motives are pure, you should not blame yourself. Here it is taken as read that your motives are sincere and genuine.

Worked Consultation:
A Romantic Dilemma

Nicole and Max had been dating for two years but put off getting married as both were involved in high-powered careers that took up a great deal of their time. They each had their own flat in London but lived close enough to enjoy the best of both worlds. Nicole, who worked for a small PR company, occasionally wondered where the relationship was going, while Max was simply too busy (and too involved) in his job as a top management consultant to give it much

thought. They spent the weekends visiting each other's family in the country and took Christmas and summer holidays together.

In February 2003 Max was asked to head up a new company in Washington, DC. He was keen to accept the promotion and invited Nicole to come with him. He did not propose marriage but suggested they live together instead.

Nicole knew that to go to Washington with Max would mean taking a big risk, both professionally and personally. She decided to consult the Plum Blossom Oracle and chose to do so at the hour of the dragon – 8 am on Sunday 16 February 2003. She phrased her question as follows:

Will it be beneficial for me to follow Max and live with him in Washington?

Nicole used the Early Heaven arrangement method to formulate the hexagram.

Lower Trigram

Nicole used the time of the consultation to obtain the lower trigram (see Table 1 on page 42).

- for 8 am the hour number is 5

- for 16 the day number is 16

- for February the month number is 1

- for 2003 the year number is 8

- 5 + 16 + 1 + 8 = 30

- Dividing 30 by 8 gives 3 with a remainder of 6, so the relevant trigram under the yin pa kua arrangement is Kan (see Table 2 on page 42), whose element is water.

Upper Trigram

Nicole decided to create the upper trigram by using the words 'Max' and 'Washington', as she felt they encapsulated the essence of her dilemma. She had no qualms about giving up her job, as she was confident of finding employment fairly easily. What she needed to know was how the move would affect her relationship. Would it lead to marriage? Here are the numerical equivalents of the words (see Table 3 on page 42).

- Max is 4 + 1 + 6 = 11

- Washington is 5 + 1 + 1 + 8 + 9 + 5 + 7 + 2 + 6 + 5 = 49

- 11 + 49 = 60

- Dividing 60 by 8 gives 7 with a remainder of 4, so the equivalent trigram is Chen (see Table 2 on page 42), whose element is wood.

The Changing Line

Dividing the time numbers (see the lower trigram), which total 30, by 6 gives 5, so the changing line is line 5.

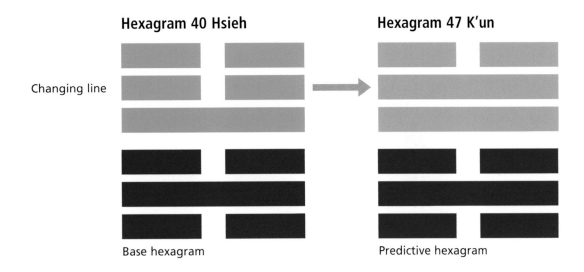

Hexagram 40 Hsieh | **Hexagram 47 K'un**

Changing line

Base hexagram | Predictive hexagram

The Base and Predictive Hexagrams

To identify the correct hexagram, refer to the table on pages 88–89. Match the upper and lower trigrams to get the hexagram number, then refer to Chapter 5.

From the upper and lower trigrams, Nicole generated the base hexagram Hsieh, which is made up of the trigram Kan below and Chen above. Here water below is producing wood above – a very auspicious hexagram. The immediate reply to Nicole's question was that the move would be both nourishing and liberating. The primary trigrams' relationship was most auspicious indeed. The nuclear trigrams were Li (fire) below and Kan (water) above and this indicated a situation where fire causes water to transform into steam energy. Although the relationship appears destructive, here the deeper meaning of the element was that the long-term effect of her move would bring her power and influence, suggesting that she could land a fabulous new job or that her relationship with Max would make her very confident and happy.

Here hexagram Hsieh was transformed into the predictive hexagram K'un as a result of the changing line 5.

The texts of the base hexagram Hsieh advised, 'If there is something to do, doing it quickly brings good fortune.' Line 5 said, 'This line suggests a positive answer to all your questions.' The oracle was strongly advising Nicole to move to Washington with Max.

The predictive hexagram caused by the changing line 5 was K'un, which suggested obstacles facing Nicole. But the hexagram also advised, 'The superior man maintains his composure and transforms adversity into good fortune.' Read closely, the texts of the hexagram seemed to suggest that staying on in London without Max would 'cause the lake to run dry'. So both hexagrams advised Nicole to move to Washington with Max.

Note: Nicole did move to Washington with Max, in the face of some opposition from her parents and some resistance from her employers. Soon after arriving, in the course of house-hunting, Max proposed. They got married shortly before moving into their new place in May. Nicole has since joined a PR firm in Washington and both she and Max have prospered at work. They are a 'power couple', continue to be very focused on their careers and are blissfully happy together.

Worked Consultation:
A Business Dilemma

Paul Lo had been successfully running his father's building construction company, Transonic, for the past six years. The company had grown slowly and steadily, but in recent months Paul had been made nervous by the spate of bad news – economic downturns, the Iraq war, bombings round the world and, early in 2003, the SARS outbreak. His business had not been adversely affected directly, as he continued to win lucrative contracts, but now he had to decide whether to expand or not. The projects on hand seemed to justify expanding, but he was worried that he might suffer if any of his clients defaulted on payments.

Paul contemplated his dilemma as he was driving to work one morning in March 2003. Along the way his attention was caught by a heavily overloaded lorry in front of him – it was carrying sand, a trail of which was spilling on to the road as the lorry crept from one set of traffic lights to the next. Paul shook his head in disgust at the carelessness of the driver, but then it occurred to him that seeing the lorry that morning might be telling him something about his dilemma. Quickly he jotted down the lorry's number plate, which was WJ 3557.

As soon as he arrived at his office, Paul decided to refer to the Plum Blossom Oracle. In business matters Paul had been successfully guided by the I Ching for several years and he was confident that the oracle would offer some insights to help him resolve his business dilemma.

Paul phrased his question this way:

Shall I invest half a million dollars buying two new cranes for the business over the coming two months?

As Paul had had many years' experience consulting the Plum Blossom Oracle, he opted for the Later Heaven arrangement method to formulate the hexagram. He decided to use the lorry's number plate to formulate the lower trigram and the numerical equivalent of his company's name to formulate the upper trigram.

Lower Trigram

Paul felt instinctively that the lorry could be used to determine the fate trigram as he was thinking of his dilemma at the precise moment when he saw it. That the lorry created strong feelings of agitation in him made him believe it was a significant sign for him to interpret, so using the number WJ 3557 he created the fate trigram for the hexagram. To do so, first he had to convert WJ into a numerical aspect (see Table 3 on page 52).

- WJ is 5 + 1 = 6

- 3 + 5 + 5 + 7 = 20

- 6 + 20 = 26

- Dividing 26 by 8 gives 3 with a remainder of 2, so the relevant trigram (the fate trigram) under the yang pa kua arrangement is Kun (see Table 2 on page 52), whose element is earth.

Upper Trigram

For the upper trigram Paul decided to use the numerical equivalent of Transonic. As he had used the oracle many times, he knew this would create the trigram Kan or water (which is why he uses the water symbol as his company logo).

- Transonic is 2 + 9 + 1 + 5 + 1 + 6 + 5 + 9 + 3 = 41

- Dividing 41 by 8 gives 5 with a remainder of 1, so the upper or subject trigram is Kan (see Table 2 on page 52), whose element is water.

The Changing Line

To obtain the changing line Paul added up the numbers of the upper and lower trigram and divided the total by 6. So:

- 26 + 41 = 67

- Dividing 67 by 6 gives 11 with a remainder of 1, so the changing line is line 1.

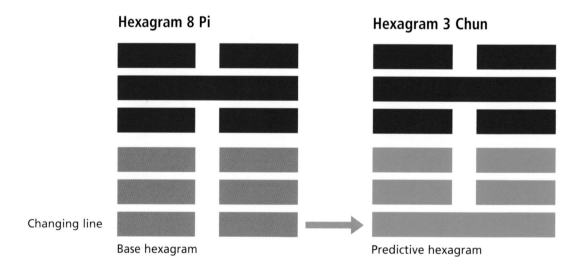

Hexagram 8 Pi   Hexagram 3 Chun

Changing line

Base hexagram   Predictive hexagram

The Base and Predictive Hexagrams

To identify the correct hexagram, refer to the table on pages 88–9. Match the upper and lower trigrams to get the hexagram number, then refer to Chapter 5.

Paul generated the base hexagram Pi, which is made up of the trigrams Kun below and Kan above. Here earth below and water above indicate water overflowing – a situation of potential danger where water just might cause misfortune. But Pi also symbolizes a 'holding together' according to the texts of the hexagrams. Paul wondered whether watching the overloaded lorry might be sending him a message that expansion could bring the company eventual benefits if he held together, but that there was also the danger that he might be biting off more than he could chew. The lorry could topple, causing disaster, so in the same way he could also be putting his company in danger. The water just might overflow perilously.

Paul also studied the nuclear trigrams and was pleasantly surprised to note that here the elements indicated earth doubled (the nuclear trigrams are Ken above and Kun below, both of which have earth for their element), suggesting ultimate good fortune. The trigrams indicated that there was good fortune in the long run.

Next Paul decided to see what the moving line said and here he noted that the I Ching answered his question directly, saying, 'You can proceed with confidence.'

Finally Paul looked at the predictive hexagram, Chun, which suggested initial hardship. Note the opening words of this trigram: '... difficulty at the start. You must look for help and learn from experience. Perseverance makes the young man superior.'

Note: Paul was certain that the Plum Blossom Oracle was asking him to proceed with the expansion. He was already aware of the risks he was taking, but by expanding at a time when business confidence was so low, he could get the extra cranes at a bargain price, thus enabling him to be more competitive. Soon after buying the new cranes (for which he had to borrow money from the bank), Paul successfully tendered for a plum job – building a new condominium project.

CHAPTER 5

Texts and Judgments

The 64 hexagrams of the I Ching offer judgments and commentaries using metaphorical statements and images. The answers to many questions lie in the imagery of the lines. Focus on the lines and you will be able to grasp the seed of all things; you might even penetrate the intentions of those who walk the earth and interact with you. Regardless of whether your question concerns something near or far, secret or profound, immediate or some time away, the answer lies within the changing and unchanging lines of the hexagrams.

The 64 Hexagrams

LOWER		Chien	Chen	Kan
Chien		1	34	5
Chen		25	51	3
Kan		6	40	29
Ken		33	62	39
Kun		12	16	8
Sun		44	32	48
Li		13	55	63
Tui		10	54	60

Ken	Kun	Sun	Li	Tui
26	11	9	14	43
27	24	42	21	17
4	7	59	64	47
52	15	53	56	31
23	2	20	35	45
18	46	57	50	28
22	36	37	30	49
41	19	61	38	58

1 Chien

Symbolizes the vital spirit of heaven

The spirit rising, vitality returning
Activity backed by heaven is full of strength
Bringing authority and attainments

The Creative: the image of heaven and symbol of pure yang energy, the sun, representing strength and firmness. Chien suggests a solid foundation and predicts an auspicious outcome. The moving lines will indicate when the outcome will materialize. Since the image is of the powerful dragon, this hexagram is to be respected. It symbolizes a strong leader, a patriarchal force whose inner strength has great substance and whose outer appearance suggests authority. At its most positive, Chien indicates a strong leader who possesses wisdom and humility. This hexagram advises the need to curb a tendency to become overly arrogant and despotic.

The I Ching says, 'There are many benefits that come from perseverance and from holding firm.' Success is certain, so be unswerving in your resolve. Trust your instincts. Heaven moves powerfully to support you for as long as you stay true to your principles and goals. If you receive this hexagram in answer to your question, the oracle is saying, 'Trust your instincts and go with the flow.' Chien is significant if you experienced a happy encounter on the day you asked the question.

The Elements
Metal interacts with metal to strengthen the resolve. Here the element is doubled and the meaning is very auspicious. It suggests movement, activity, transformation and change – all of which will lead to a beneficial outcome. Good fortune in matters of promotion, career and business or questions relating to the patriarch is indicated.

The Moving Lines
Line 1 (at the bottom): This is not a good time to act or commit to anything new. Instead prepare for something more beneficial that lies around the corner. Business and mobility appear slow in the immediate future, but relationships with friends and family stay strong. The image is of a hidden dragon, so the time has not come for you to show yourself.

Line 2: This is a time of great development. You will get help from your superiors or from someone older than you. Be alert for excellent assignments, jobs or opportunities that are coming your way. Students will excel in their examinations and succeed in winning scholarships. Women can become prosperous through marriage, or achieve success if they are starting new jobs. The image is of a frolicking dragon in the field and the advice is, 'It benefits to see the great man.'

Line 3: Be cautious. This is a time when your success is evident. There will be pressures and a feeling of inadequacy. You will feel the weight of responsibilities and expectations that come with success. Relationships will suffer because you are distracted and stressed. In climbing the ladder of success, your abilities are being challenged. Short-term prospects do not look promising, but patience will bring its own rewards.

Line 4: A time of transition and decision, when you must choose between divergent paths. You could be in a dilemma about something. There is no way to know which is the superior path, but there is some good short-term luck. The I Ching advises that you be watchful. Be wary and do not be too trusting. Women will enjoy good luck. The image is of the hungry dragon but the advice is there is 'no blame'.

Line 5: Excellent good fortune. Mentors appear on the horizon and bring power, progress and opportunities. There may be promotion, but beware of lingering jealousies under the veneer of smiles. Do not let success go to your head – it can cause your downfall.

Line 6: Arrogance leads to trouble. Pause and think of anyone you may have offended without intending to. There is loss of friendship indicated. On a happier note, you will meet someone with whom you could start a serious relationship. Marriage could come from the encounter, so be alert. The image here is of the arrogant dragon who may have cause to repent. So if you get this line the I Ching is advising you to soften and be less overbearing.

2 K'un

Symbolizes a multiplicity of things

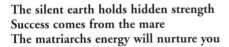

The silent earth holds hidden strength
Success comes from the mare
The matriarchs energy will nurture you

The Receptive: K'un signifies earth, the mother and the purest of yin energy. Yielding overcomes strength, and endurance brings resilience. The image of the mare belonging to the earth complements that of the dragon belonging to heaven. Both are images that predict success, and while Chien manifests the best of one's spiritual potential, K'un manifests the best of one's material reality.

This hexagram favours those in supporting roles. It encourages one to look for a leader. To succeed, allow yourself to be guided. Discard any feelings of partisanship or politics. Rise above factionalism and favouritism. Be like a mother and manifest the largesse of your inner heart. This will bring you ultimate triumph. Great success is indicated by this hexagram and benefits arise from perseverance. There are peace, harmony and good fortune.

The sighting of a coloured bird preceding this consultation indicates good news is coming your way. A red bird signifies a new opportunity. A yellow bird means spiritual growth that brings greater happiness. A blue or black bird indicates wealth. If the bird flies from the south or west it brings enormous good fortune.

The Elements
Here the interaction is earth doubled: in other words, there is a good supply of an element that indicates solid foundation and safety. K'un is an auspicious hexagram.

The Moving Lines
Line 1 (at the bottom): Beware of jealousy that sends little arrows of poison your way. Deflect them by not responding. Or take action to block them. Women who feature in the consultation will bring prosperity and happiness to their family and employees. Follow your instincts. Protect yourself at work with the image of a rooster.

Line 2: Everything benefits. There is a promotion coming your way. There is also recognition, which will open the door to prosperity. All is well in your life. Despite signs to the contrary, the relationships in your life are fine. There is no need to worry. As long as you are true in your dealings with others, the indications are that you are on the right track. You can proceed with confidence.

Line 3: This line suggests a time for cautious advancement. Fuel your ambition and do not be afraid to accept promotions that are offered, but stay humble. A quiet acceptance brings greater benefits. This line suggests magnificent good fortune hidden within an ordinary position. You will find peace and happiness if you keep a low profile.

Line 4: This line advises that you stay watchful and alert. If you act, you must do so with caution. Read the fine print if you are signing agreements. Delay responding to propositions. Give yourself time to reflect. Use delaying tactics if you must. Things may not be what they seem, so allow time for the situation to unfold. But be diplomatic.

Line 5: Everything goes smoothly. There is added income in what you contemplate. It is a time of excellent energy. Whatever you do will benefit you, especially if you wear yellow. Better yet, wear a yellow stone such as citrine or amber. This line is one of the most blessed of the I Ching's answers. It always heralds great good fortune. The sighting of a lame dog or accident preceding this consultation is not a good sign as it negates the excellent outcome. The sighting of anything yellow is an excellent sign as it confirms and reinforces the oracle.

Line 6: Expect danger. This line is a warning that you might be manoeuvred out of a job or assignment. There could be a lawsuit with someone previously friendly to you. Respond with humility. If you fight you will lose. If you are waiting for news, what emerges may not be beneficial for you. Exam results are uninspiring. It is better to let the hard times blow over before taking the next step. If you get this line go outside and look up at the sky. If it is blue and the weather is good it suggests you can successfully overcome any loss or bad news. Bright sunshine means misfortune will transform into good fortune. Dark clouds and rain suggest that you must be very careful. Protect yourself with amulet coins – something made of metal that can keep bad luck exhausted.

3 Chun

Symbolizes difficulty getting started

Clouds and thunder symbolize difficulty at the start
You must look for help and learn from experience
Perseverance makes a young man superior …
and successful

This hexagram suggests difficulty, confusion and obstacles at the start of undertakings – either in business, in a new job or in a relationship. Do not be discouraged, because the situation will improve, even though it takes time. The I Ching suggests that difficulty always precedes success. If the obstacles facing you appear difficult to overcome, look outside yourself for assistance. This hexagram suggests the need to reorganize your set-up and rethink your strategy. Planning is important at this stage. In short, go back to the drawing board.

Do not be stubborn or force the issue. Do not be too proud to ask for help. The oracle is suggesting that you lack the experience and knowledge to cope. This is a moment when humility brings better results than arrogance. Help will be forthcoming if you ask the right people. Be encouraged by the knowledge that great success can be yours. The oracle says, 'The superior man brings order out of chaos.'

If what caught your eye today denotes growth – for example, a little bird learning to fly – the imagery is auspicious. If, on the other hand, you were confronted with overgrown grass or had problems getting to work, then the indications are less auspicious.

The Elements

Li (fire) is above Chen (wood). Here the relationship is both productive and exhaustive. The lower trigram is producing and is exhausted by the top trigram, indicating initial difficulty. If you look at the nuclear trigrams, you see Ken over Kun – mountain over big earth. The inner trigrams indicate great harmony, meaning hidden success.

The Moving Lines

Line 1 (at the bottom): Good fortune is indicated. Careers and relationships will enjoy good progress. This is a time not to be held back by doubts but to move ahead with confidence. Proceed decisively. Surround yourself with friends who will help you. Keep your goal constantly in sight.

Line 2: Many difficulties and hindrances are indicated. You need to be very patient as obstacles crop up. Despite this, it is a good time for getting married or starting a new job. It is important that you do not remain alone now. You need friends around you, but trust only people you know. Unexpected lifelines from unknown sources can bring heartache and grief later on. If you saw a dead rat, a dead snake or a dead cat run over on the road, it is a good sign, indicating that the major misfortune is already behind you.

Line 3: Refrain from taking further action. Hold back, because any premature move could bring disaster. You do not have enough experience and could get lost if you attempt to move ahead into unknown territory. Students will encounter obstacles. Plans cannot succeed.

Line 4: Good fortune in everything. Marriage prospects look promising if you are already dating someone. Those who are pursuing some specific goal can also succeed. At work there is the prospect for promotion and recognition. So whatever it is that you are working on, proceed with confidence. Do not allow false pride or false modesty to immobilize you. Actions speak louder than words. This becomes a certainty if you saw something auspicious in the two hours prior to making this consultation or you received a happy phone call, or someone sends flowers or a gift to your house.

Line 5: Good fortune in small things is indicated by this moving line, which also warns you to be alert to misfortune in big matters. So if you are thinking of moving ahead in a large endeavour or going on a long journey, it is better to delay. Short journeys and small projects will attract success.

Line 6: Be very careful as this line indicates extreme misfortune. There is some kind of setback associated with your question. It is a good idea to buy a protective amulet.

4 Meng

Symbolizes getting caught

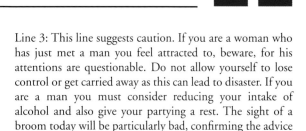

**Water at the base of the mountain suggests
Ignorance of the way ahead – in time, however,
A teacher shows the way
And then the path becomes clear**

Meng suggests it is time for you to seek a teacher, but your attitude should reflect genuine humility and a serious intention. Perhaps you are too playful. To grow as a person, you must have a sincere desire to assuage your thirst for knowledge and to learn from those who have experience and wisdom. Seek counsel from only the best, so your arrogant, youthful mind will respect them. When you have found someone suitable, trust their words. Once there is mistrust, even the most brilliant teacher soon becomes as silent as the mountains. When questions get repeated again and again, in an atmosphere of doubt, there can be no wise counsel. Hence this hexagram is addressed to those with an immature attitude. If you get this hexagram examine your motives.

The Elements
Ken (earth) is above Li (fire), so the lower trigram is producing the upper. It suggests the potential for growth. The inner nuclear trigrams are Kun above Chen, or earth above wood. Here the lower nuclear trigram is destroying the upper trigram, suggesting the potential for disaster in the long term, hence the need to be sincere and genuine.

The Moving Lines
Line 1 (at the bottom): Develop discipline to succeed, discarding playfulness and carelessness. It is a time to back down. Do not be arrogant. Instead adopt the demeanour of one who wishes to learn, then success will come. Remember that character takes time to build. This line indicates good news for students, who can look forward to greater achievements. Some misunderstandings are, however, indicated for those with relationship concerns.

Line 2: This moving line suggests excellent indications of a coming marriage. If you are already married it suggests a child may soon be born. This is a peaceful and satisfying period when powerful friends open new opportunities for you. This is a good line and also indicates a son who has a strong sense of responsibility. If you saw a pair or a family of birds any time two hours before or after the consultation it suggests very good marriage and descendants luck. Sightings of other auspicious symbols are indications of good fortune. If you dreamed of flying or birds it is also a good sign.

Line 3: This line suggests caution. If you are a woman who has just met a man you feel attracted to, beware, for his attentions are questionable. Do not allow yourself to lose control or get carried away as this can lead to disaster. If you are a man you must consider reducing your intake of alcohol and also give your partying a rest. The sight of a broom today will be particularly bad, confirming the advice to be careful of your new friend.

Line 4: There is confusion and humiliation. This line suggests that you are going through troubled times. Neither promotion nor fresh opportunities are possible. There are simply a thousand obstacles blocking your path to success, so try not to get entangled and be warned against trying new places. It is a good idea to carry some protective amulet made of metal inside your pocket or handbag.

Line 5: This is a lucky line as it indicates good fortune. Despite your inexperience and the mistakes you make, you can have success. Childlike folly nevertheless brings good fortune! Success comes from taking the advice of an older person. This is the only really good line of the hexagram. It is strengthened if at the moment of consultation someone turns on the radio or TV, thereby imbuing the reading with powerful yang energy.

Line 6: This line suggests a many misunderstandings, quarrels and even legal entanglements such as lawsuits. You may find yourself having to discipline or punish someone. Refrain from excessive anger and be patient with youthful exuberance. For students this line indicates an auspicious moment when results are favourable and goals can be achieved.

5 Hsu

Symbolizes waiting

Clouds in the heaven suggest a time of waiting
Rain comes, but only when the wind dragon blows

This is a period when opportunity has not yet arrived. Everything must therefore stay as ideas in the head. There is danger and uncertainty, so you need to think carefully and prepare yourself. This hexagram, which suggests waiting, also indicates nourishment, which is a good sign. There is thus a strong element of preparation in the advice given. It benefits to 'cross the great water', which means that whatever idea you have in mind will be beneficial in the long run. It has the chance to succeed.

The oracle advises you to analyse your situation calmly. There is a need for courage when confronted with seeming adversity. Remember, this hexagram is saying that, despite difficulties, all is not lost. It advises you to stay cheerful and joyous. Why? Because clouds in the sky mean that soon it will rain, and with rain comes good fortune. You need only wait. When the time is right the solution – help or answers – will come.

The Elements

Kan (water) is above Chien (metal). Here metal produces water, creating the promise of good fortune. The nuclear trigrams are Li (fire) above Tui (metal), with the upper trigram in a destructive relationship with the lower. There is indication of some hidden danger. The oracle suggests you wait and see what happens. Waiting brings good fortune, while acting precipitously could create a situation of danger.

The Moving Lines

Line 1 (at the bottom): This line suggests that you must consolidate as a strategy. Danger and bad times are still around. If you act now you will only waste your strength. Better to conserve your energy.

Line 2: Agitation and gossip cause aggravation and bad feelings. It is a highly stressful time of disagreements and misunderstandings. The oracle advises an attitude of calm. You can also take comfort from the knowledge that good fortune is coming. There is no need to react to bad-mouthing as it will dissipate on its own.

Line 3: Be cautious, especially if you are embarking on a new journey. Take all necessary precautions when travelling in a foreign country. Do not trust strangers and be particularly careful of handling packages. This line also indicates someone harmful coming into your life, someone who can cause you distress and loss. If you awoke feeling a sense of dread, or with pains in your back, it confirms that someone you met recently or will meet over the next few days will create the cause of your unhappiness. It is a good idea to wear protective amulets to dispel the influence of harmful people.

Line 4: Your current situation is causing you stress, and with good reason. It is a time of extreme danger when what awaits you could be a matter of life and death. The oracle predicts bloodshed, a falling into a pit of violence. In relationships the situation cannot improve and it is necessary to accept this. If you get this changing line it is telling you to avoid taking any action, as anything you do will only aggravate the situation. It is vital to stay low key and be quiet. Do not wear red, as this will only make the situation worse; better to wear black or blue.

Line 5: Good fortune is coming soon. The oracle suggests a financial windfall. There is also a successful acquisition of new property. For those in relationships, marriage is possible. This is the best line in this hexagram, as the indications appear to be excellent. Perseverance brings good fortune. For those who saw any of the love symbols – mandarin ducks, the dragon or phoenix – marriage is a possibility. Those who saw a real estate magazine or a property they liked may soon be considering investing in a new property.

Line 6: You will be playing host to three unexpected guests. Treat them well, for they bring you opportunities that have the potential to ripen into great good fortune. There is no need to go overboard in your generosity, but respect their opinions and advice. The oracle suggests that things will appear very bad initially, with relief coming only at the last minute. So wait for the happy turn of events. For those who have been plagued by a severe problem relating to their work or the ill health of some family member, this line promises relief. The message is considerably strengthened if you should see auspicious symbols in the course of the week that follows.

6 Sung
Symbolizes conflict

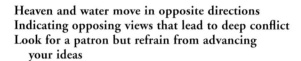

Heaven and water move in opposite directions
Indicating opposing views that lead to deep conflict
Look for a patron but refrain from advancing
your ideas

This hexagram suggests disagreements that stem from opposing views either in your mind or between friends and colleagues. Inner conflict often creates the cause for disputes, disagreements and sometimes open hostility. The forces that are unleashed will be difficult to reconcile. Such differences can manifest themselves in a number of ways – between older and younger generations, between those who want war and those who believe in peaceful conflict resolution, between being cautious and throwing caution to the winds.

If you get this hexagram, the advice is to maintain the status quo. This will bring good fortune because differences can then be resolved with the passage of time. This is not a time to be egotistical and high-handed. Look to someone older and wiser to settle your differences. Refrain from proceeding in your course of action until conflicts have been resolved. When unity does not prevail success is hard to come by. For love relationships, the oracle predicts conflicts that might be hard to sort out. Better to refrain from saying too much, because words have a way of making things worse. For those looking for a change of career or a new job, this hexagram does not promise anything positive. There is inner and outer conflict. Nothing works.

The Elements
Chien (metal) is above Kan (water). Heaven is being exhausted by water moving in a separate direction. This hexagram bodes ill for the patriarch. The nuclear trigrams are Sun (wood) above Li (fire), so the upper trigram is again exhausted. The elements suggest conflict that will exhaust all parties.

The Moving Lines
Line 1 (at the bottom): Gossip, lawsuits and disaster await you if you get this line and persist in your course of action. Ignore attempts to annoy you and all outstanding issues will be resolved. If you proceed with a strategy of litigation or confrontation you will lose. Here the oracle is suggesting that your adversary has better luck than you, so it is better to let go. This round is not yours. He who runs away lives to fight another day.

Line 2: The oracle advises a retreat. Avoid direct and open confrontation. Do not fight your adversary, who is much too strong. You do not have the luck to win. A better strategy is one of reconciliation and the adoption of a peaceful attitude. If you hold steady in this resolve you will regain your equilibrium and the situation will stabilize.

Line 3: This is no time to be ambitious. Any plans for expansion should be put on hold. It is also wise to take a humble attitude and desist from being arrogant. You should wait for a less hostile scenario.

Line 4: Losses will definitely be recovered, as this line indicates that luck is on your side. But you will taste good fortune only if you refrain from direct conflict. Do nothing and let fate take its course. The peaceful way will achieve happiness.

Line 5: A powerful and influential person will help you, opening new ways for you to move ahead. This is an excellent line to get in answer to your concerns. Hold steadfast and carry on: 'It benefits to see the great man.' The oracle urges you to trust the man who will decide on whatever is causing you stress. Conflict will be resolved to your advantage. This line brings supreme good fortune. Noting everyday things going smoothly for you – your journey to work, for example – will reinforce the prediction of this line.

Line 6: Your luck is mixed, so there will be good and bad news, success and failure. The scenario here is of battles won and then new conflicts arising. The oracle stresses the bitterness of having to contend with one struggle after another. Better, then, to not get stressed out. For students the line predicts excellent grades, but there could be some negative developments as well.

7 Shih

Symbolizes the mass of humanity

**Earth above and water below indicates a situation of danger
But there are also obedience and discipline – suggesting an army –
A mass of people whose power is invisible and controlled**

Water and earth are powerful forces. Water can overflow but earth can subdue it. The single yang line indicates a strong and powerful leader who controls the masses. This hexagram suggests a gathering of people who are inspired by leadership and charismatic qualities. The image here is of an efficient fighting force, a well-disciplined army. There is one clear leader and the rest are subordinates. The challenge is to keep the people in line so there is no scope for chaos and anarchy. This hexagram suggests that you can overcome your enemies and also any competition that may be threatening you.

If you are in business and your question concerns this, the hexagram suggests that you need to take another look at your organization's structure. In the family, it points to the need for the head of the family to exert himself, otherwise things could fall apart.

The Elements
Kun (earth) is above Kan (water). This is a situation where earth controls water. The relationship is potentially dangerous but under control. The nuclear trigrams have earth above and wood below, which suggests someone or something strong pushing through into a position of power. This signifies the hidden force, which can be positive or negative but is clandestine. The suggestion here is to watch your back, for the nuclear trigrams indicate a new unknown adversary who could challenge your authority.

The Moving Lines
Line 1 (at the bottom): This line indicates a need for order and discipline in order to avoid misfortune. Success comes only with proper organization and structured activity, especially when many people are acting together.

Line 2: This line indicates that you will receive a great honour from someone powerful, such as a decoration of some kind. This unexpected recognition of your qualities will be beneficial to your performance. You can rejoice. If you also notice a red bird or see the image of a horse today, this definitely indicates that you will shortly receive some high honour and recognition.

Line 3: This line indicates that someone may have succeeded in usurping your position, causing misfortune to befall either you and your company or you and your family. It suggests a third party coming in to upset the delicate balance of control you exert, so the indications are inauspicious. If you see a wild animal or dream of a predator attacking you, it strengthens the prediction.

Line 4: This line suggests that now is the time to retreat. If there is an orderly unwinding of actions and events you will find the exercise beneficial, otherwise there is grave danger to either you and your family or you and your company.

Line 5: This line suggests some kind of prize or attainment that is within reach, but to get it you need a good strategy and effective planning. Everyone must act in concert, as teamwork is what will bring you victory. If your management is lacking you will taste failure. Only good leadership can lead to success.

Line 6: This line indicates resolution of an outstanding issue and also victory for you of a substantial kind, so there is cause for celebration and rejoicing. But the oracle also offers a word of advice. Do not become careless. Guard against arrogance. The I Ching reminds you that all things change and good fortune can transform into misfortune. The superior man maintains his composure and stays humble and well grounded.

8 Pi

Symbolizes a banding together

**Water above and earth below indicates holding
 together**
Harmony precedes a union
And union brings good fortune

Here the image of water above earth denotes
a bonding, indicating the possibility of a merger, a
situation in which harmony and cooperation
prevail. The single yang line is in a high position –
strong and generous – so this hexagram suggests
good fortune and harmony for those wishing to
get married, as well as for those who are
negotiating a merger or joint venture. It also
indicates great prosperity and good fortune,
especially for those who proceed with sincerity. It is not
advisable to hesitate, as lack of confidence will trigger bad
luck. Trust your feelings on anything that may be engaging
your mind.

The Elements

Earth below and water above are in conflict. The nuclear
trigrams are Ken and Kun, both earth. Earth doubled
suggests inner calmness and good fortune, so in the long
term the indications seem auspicious.

The Moving Lines

Line 1 (at the bottom): You can proceed with confidence
if you obtain this changing line. You will receive help
from friends and even get an unexpected promotion. At the
same time there will be other opportunities opening up for
you. If you see a colourful bird, this will reinforce the
prediction for you.

Line 2: Help comes to you from your superiors if you get
this line. Scholarships and recognition are strongly
indicated. Women asking about love will find good
husbands, and lovers will turn their thoughts to getting
married. Your aspirations are achievable. Use a catalyst to
get things moving. Buy yourself a crystal to enhance the chi
of your inner wishes. Time is on your side.

Line 3: This line indicates that you are in danger of forming
a union with an unsuitable person or unsuitable people
who will be bad for you, as there could be wasted
opportunities and loss of money. There is danger from the
green-eyed monster as others watch you with jealous eyes.
There is also some danger to your health. If you are in a
relationship with a sweetheart or business partner, it is
wise to move slowly and be watchful. Do not be too eager
to be trusting.

Line 4: This line offers excellent indications for success. You
can proceed with your intentions but your motives should
be pure. Watch your mind.

Line 5: There is promise of a great honour being bestowed
on you. Good fortune comes in large measure and
everything in your life proceeds smoothly. You will find
happiness with your current beloved. This is a good time to
think about taking the relationship a step further – perhaps
marriage. And for those already married who are in an
unhappy situation, this is a good time to start afresh. If you
see an auspicious object, such as a pair of birds, it confirms
that you will find happiness in love. If you spot a single bird
it is time to move on, as something or someone is just
around the corner. If you had a happy dream the message
of this changing line is reinforced.

Line 6: There is a misfortune indicated by this line. Trials
and tribulations come in battalions and there are
indications of threats to your health, so take care. This line
is telling you that you lack support and quarrels will come
at you from many quarters. Wear a protective amulet and
try to overcome the quarrelling chi that seems to be
surrounding you. Wear red to strengthen your chi. You
could place the image of a dragon tortoise (a creature with
the head of a dragon and body of a tortoise) behind you at
work to increase your support.

9 Hsiao Ch'u

Symbolizes small involvement

The wind blowing across the skies
Suggests a taming of the small powers
The superior man adjusts his demeanour
In small ways … but it is sufficient

This hexagram implies rest and preparation. Sun above and Chien below signify fine weather above the heaven. This imagery suggests that there are good things on the way, but they come in small measures. The wind here is gentle and soft, so the news is good.

The nuclear trigrams are also auspicious as there is fire hidden in the hexagram, as symbolized by the trigram Li. This indicates sunshine as well as a brightness and hidden yang energy. And the lower nuclear trigram Tui suggests a joyousness. The texts are thus indicating good fortune. But the element is metal, so there is a cap placed on your good fortune. There will be limits to your success and to the good news. The wind blows clouds to cover the sun and soon there is rain. So the hexagram indicates a certain amount of difficulty, although eventually there will be success. This is not a remarkable hexagram but it does suggest a steady improvement of fortunes.

The Elements

Chien (metal) below Sun (wood) means that the two elements are in conflict. Here wood above is being hurt by metal. We can also interpret this as metal transforming wood. The nuclear trigrams are fire above metal, also a situation of control and conflict.

The Moving Lines

Line 1 (at the bottom): The line indicates peace and harmony, but there is an urgent need to make some decisions and this can pose some difficulty. The oracle advises contemplation before deciding and then it is necessary to be decisive. When careful thought precedes action there is good fortune. Success awaits just around the corner. There is cause for smiling. This is a good line.

Line 2: Good influences bring good fortune. You can look forward to being promoted soon, because the right people have observed your fine performance. If you receive phone calls today from unexpected friends you have not heard from it is a sign of good news coming.

Line 3: You might be having marital problems or your relationship with a loved one may not be going well, so be prepared for some setbacks and unhappiness. Separations and a break-up of family are indicated. This is a sad line. I recommend wearing a strong amulet to overcome this period and carrying a mirror inside your bag. Going away for a short time will ease the situation.

Line 4: Friends stand by and verbalize their support for you. There is no reason to worry as you have hidden allies who are working on your behalf. They will bring you a series of small successes and life becomes rather pleasant.

Line 5: You can rest easy as cooperation from your friends and colleagues is definitely forthcoming. Your work will also be successful and you will make important gains in your career and projects. This is a good time for socializing and networking.

Line 6: If you get this line you should be wary of being ambushed or cornered. Slowly retreat and withdraw as there could be some troubles ahead. If you are nimble and quick you have the heaven luck to overcome a potential setback.

10 Lu

Symbolizes smug self-confidence

Treading on the tail of the tiger
Is like the vulnerable placed next to the strong
Fortify your thinking and go with the flow
This reflects the nature of things ...

This hexagram advises you to recognize that the reality of the human condition is that people are born unequal. Heaven and the lake indicated in the trigrams of this hexagram demonstrate a difference of elevation. Accepting the universal inequality of mankind will ensure there is neither envy nor frustration. But having accepted the inevitability of social ranking in society, you should look within, to the inner worth of mankind, as well.

This hexagram also describes the situation within a family or corporation and addresses the need to bow to discipline and to your elders. Here the lower trigram, Tui, stands for the gentle youngest daughter (someone young and inexperienced), while the upper trigram is Chien, which stands for the father. The oracle is advising obedience to someone older. Youth should give way to experience. Tui is also the tiger and the lake, both of which are the source of potential danger. To avoid being bitten or falling into the lake, you must be careful.

The Elements
Both the trigrams are metal, which is auspicious as the trigrams reinforce each other. The nuclear trigrams are Li (fire) below Sun (wood), a productive sequence as wood produces fire. Both trigrams indicate women: Li is the middle daughter and Sun the eldest daughter. The hexagram here thus indicates a man with three daughters.

The Moving Lines
Line 1 (at the bottom): This line suggests it is beneficial to continue, as you can expect success and promotion. There is also money luck and good fortune waiting to be tapped. This line is reinforced if your observations during the day are also auspicious – for example, if you passed a bank van or a lorry loaded with produce.

Line 2: Caution will bring you better results than impulsive action. For those undecided about a cause of action, the advice is to retire and not proceed. The coming weeks are best spent resting rather than working. The oracle does not recommend action of any kind.

Line 3: This is a dangerous time for you and, despite what you may have dreamed or encountered today, nothing is what it seems. Watch out for people with evil intentions. They will create unexpected conflicts and even a loss of money. You could be staring misfortune in the face in that you could lose your job and position, and there will be spiteful gossip about you. Wear an amulet and make certain you carry a small rooster image inside your pocket or bag (such images are said to be excellent at 'pecking away at troublemakers').

Line 4: Disaster and troubles threaten to overwhelm you as one piece of bad news follows another. The image is of a tiger turning nasty after you step on its tail. If you see an image of a tiger, note if its mouth is open (open-mouthed tigers are said to be a dangerous sign) or closed (in which case it is not so deadly). For some this line could be indicating stress in the marriage, so tread carefully. For students this line indicates good fortune and high grades or good exam results are within your capability.

Line 5: The oracle advises you to go slow. Do not rush, as this causes you to become careless. Hard work is not recognized and there is no reward yet that is forthcoming. Whatever success you meet with is limited in its scope. Wait for another time to gain the recognition you seek.

Line 6: This line indicates great good fortune, so you can expect good news. Whatever it is you are working on will bring success and lead to more money, even more property. You have good reason to be confident. Those in love will also meet with happiness, as your loved one is sincere. Those applying for scholarships will succeed and those applying for new positions will receive an excellent job offer.

11 Tai

Symbolizes rising above adversity

**Peace comes when the natural order prevails
Yin above yang, Kun above Chien,
Reflect the ultimate harmony of the cosmos
Heaven and earth unite – bringing peace
And contentment**

This is my favourite hexagram, symbolizing in my mind the perfect balance of yin and yang, a state of harmony, peace and well-being. It is an excellent hexagram, suggesting that all is well in your world, whether you realize it or not. In the poetry of the I Ching, the Receptive mother chi moves downwards while lying above, and the Creative moves upward while staying below. This reflects the natural order of things, so their respective influences meet in harmony. As a result all things bloom and prosper.

This hexagram indicates small luck departing and big luck approaching. At a personal level, it can stand for an awakening, a realization of the things that matter in your life. Within you the light is lit and the darkness of yin is pushed out. Light becomes influential, illuminating all that you do with powerful yang essence. When all that is good within occupies your core it is in control and induces change for the better. It is like having the spirit of heaven ruling on earth, within mankind. We lose our animal nature and the divine in us takes precedence. If you obtain this hexagram, open your eyes to the overwhelming profusion of images, situations and phenomena that take on significance simply because you have noticed them. This signifies the controlling nature of your mind. In this period of peace in your life, what you ultimately become depends on what you make of the skills you have and the attitudes and aspirations that drive you.

The Elements
Chien (metal) below Kun (earth) indicates a productive relationship suggesting peace and goodwill. The nuclear trigrams of Tui (wood) below Chen (metal) indicate a destructive relationship suggesting that the inner core holds the potential for self-destruction. If you get this hexagram and want to ensure the good times continue, wear yellow or red to control the metal energy.

The Moving Lines
Line 1 (at the bottom): Cooperation brings great prosperity and happiness. This line indicates that at work your boss is impressed with you and at home your partner loves you. In school your teacher has great expectations of you. The good news is that you will be able to fulfil all expectations.

Line 2: Retreat. There is support from a powerful and influential mentor who brings you great success and opens important doorways to opportunities. If you obtain this line be on the lookout for your benefactor, who is either coming into or has already come into your life. If you are unable to identify him, carry a coin amulet or place a large metallic object such as a windchime in the north-west corner of your workplace.

Line 3: Whatever problems you may currently be experiencing are superficial and can be wiped away with ease. There is no need to worry as everything works out.

Line 4: Be careful about starting new ventures as they could fail. Wait for a year and focus instead on what you are doing now. If you encounter auspicious signals, it simply means you should continue to keep your eyes open. It is not telling you to act.

Line 5: This line indicates a time of great good fortune. It suggests that everything will work brilliantly for you and all projects will succeed. Prospects for marriage are excellent and money flows in. Those at school or in college can look forward to maintaining excellent grades.

Line 6: This line suggests a bad time when slander, gossip and hostility make your life miserable. If you respond to these poisoned arrows with kindness and compassion, you will come through this period. Also wear red for enhanced energy levels that will make it easier for you to cope.

12 P'i

Symbolizes stagnation

Chien above is strength while Kun below is yielding
This is no longer the natural order
Stagnation results and so, alas, poverty prevails

In this hexagram the yin and yang of Kun and Chien are in the wrong locations. Chien, which signifies heaven, has come to the top, drawing further away, while Kun, the earth, is below, so it sinks further into the depths. This hexagram thus suggests a drawing apart, causing decline to set in: in other words, stagnation, with things coming to a standstill. So here the greatness departs, while the smallness approaches. There is disharmony, confusion and disorder. This line also suggests poverty and hard times. Strength above and weakness below indicates easy collapse and a lack of foundation.

The dark power resides within the core, while the light is outside and it dissipates. Inferior people are on the rise. The superior man has to stay silent and keep his own counsel, hiding his inner worth from the world. This hexagram is advising that the time is dangerous for you. This is also not the moment to be a hero. Mistrust is widespread and the fundamentals of human relationships are out of sync.

This is a warning hexagram. It tells you not to succumb to temptation, greed and avarice. There is no such thing as a free lunch and dazzling offers often carry hidden expectations. Instead, work hard and keep a low profile. Diligence creates its own rewards.

The Elements

Metal above earth indicates an exhaustive relationship. The nuclear trigrams are Sun (wood) above Ken (earth), a destructive relationship. The elements are thus suggesting adversity and difficulty.

The Moving Lines

Line 1 (at the bottom): Take care. Be on the lookout for bad people coming into your life as they will bring disharmony and trouble.

Line 2: Again, be cautious and circumspect. Nothing is at it seems. The time is not good for you. Neither success nor recognition is possible at this stage.

Line 3: There is the possibility that you could suffer some humiliation. Bear with failure and accept that you could be the fall guy. Wait for a more auspicious time to act. Neither success nor promotion is possible.

Line 4: This is a good line in an otherwise bad scenario. It indicates that, despite the disharmony and hostility, you have friends who will rally round you. Small successes are possible. There could even be an unexpected windfall.

Line 5: This line indicates light at the end of the tunnel as the bad times are about to finish. Rivals will at least become silent and bad luck now transforms into good, so you will make unexpected gains and reap some small rewards. If you see butterflies it suggests that a transformation is taking place – and if a butterfly enters into your home it is even more auspicious, meaning there will be helpful people coming to assist you.

Line 6: The bad times have come to an end. What has failed now succeeds. If you have been ill, you will get better. Where before someone has been spurning your advances, now the hand of friendship is extended. Again the sighting of colourful butterflies is an exceptionally good sign.

13 T'ung Jen

Symbolizes people who have affinity with each other

A fellowship of honourable men
Can change the world

This hexagram represents a group of people working effectively together. The trigrams denote brightness shining strongly in the heaven, indicating clarity and strength. Chien above and Li below stand for heaven above and a bright light below. The energy of brightness moves upward and this indicates an illumination of the skies. It is a good sign. The lines are also solid and strong except for a single yielding line. This suggests a yielding nature among many firm opinions.

The Elements
Metal above fire is potentially destructive as fire destroys metal. The nuclear trigrams also indicate Chien (metal) above, but Sun (wood) below, and this too is a destructive relationship as wood is destroyed by metal. The elements are offering a warning that there just might be too much brightness, too much yang energy. So it is advisable to lower expectations and temper one's enthusiasm a little.

The Moving Lines
Line 1 (at the bottom): This line suggests that there is a good opportunity. A long journey is indicated and everyone works well together. The cooperation is real. If you are thinking of getting married it is a good time. If you are considering a joint venture your partners will work well with you.

Line 2: This line indicates basic disagreements between you and your potential partner(s). Conflicting opinions can lead to trouble when both sides stay dogmatic and stubborn. Frustration will set in and then there can be little success. So this could be a time to spend some time apart. If it is a business venture you are asking about then the answer is to shelve the idea. It is a non-starter.

Line 3: This line suggests difficulty for three days, three months or three years. It depends on the nature of your question. If you are asking about something long term then troubles will beset you for three years, but if you are asking about something relatively minor then the difficulty will last only three days.

Line 4: New responsibilities will lead to success and if you are involved with property you will prosper. Work carefully and avoid careless mistakes. If you are careful you will catch the eye of someone important.

Line 5: This line offers good and bad news. The good news is that you will be recognized and there is also some short-lived fame and fortune. The bad news is you will attract some envy and gossip, which will dissipate if you can ignore it.

Line 6: If you get this line you should not change your job or your sweetheart now. Any change will lead to heartbreak and unhappiness. So stay contented with what you presently have.

14 Ta Yu

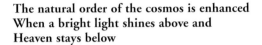

Symbolizes having great possessions

**The natural order of the cosmos is enhanced
When a bright light shines above and
Heaven stays below**

Great riches, wealth and prosperity – here is a hexagram where the bright and glorious Li trigram is on top while Chien is below, reflecting the natural order of things enhanced. The two trigrams indicate strength and clarity united. And the weak yin line is in the place of honour – the fifth line. This indicates modesty and humility amidst great riches and thus there is possession in great measure. Power manifests itself in a controlled way and this can only bring supreme success and great wealth. What is achieved will thus be on a very grand scale.

The Elements
Fire above metal is apparently a destructive relationship, yet here the metal is forged into something precious by the upward flowing power of fire. The nuclear trigrams indicate Chien below and Tui above, both of which symbolize metal energy. Here is metal combined, indicating a powerful inner core. The good fortune is thus real and has substance and longevity as well.

The Moving Lines
Line 1 (at the bottom): If you are feeling frustrated and have problems at work, walk away, resign. Your luck is shining and something better will come round in no time. The advice is the same if you are in an unhappy relationship. Unless you are single you cannot attract another mate;

and if you are trapped in a depressing marriage, take a holiday to contemplate the next step.

Line 2: If you obtain this line all your worries about the competition are unnecessary. You will experience success and can outdo everyone. There is no need to react or respond, just continue doing what you are good at. Your luck is at a high level.

Line 3: Those of you who are rich will get richer, working people will be promoted and anyone who gets this line will experience at least a small level of success.

Line 4: Success is definitely assured. Whatever you are engaged in at present you will receive good news. Those with illnesses will recover. Lost objects will be found. Travels and meetings will yield good results. Quarrels and misunderstandings will be resolved.

Line 5: This line indicates powerful good fortune. Humility brings honours. Yielding attracts praise and recognition. You have every reason to be confident in whatever you undertake. Give to charity today and your good fortune will be enhanced even more.

Line 6: This line suggests that you are 'blessed by heaven'. Everything will be beneficial. There are prosperity and high honours. You will receive a promotion and good influences come your way. Your health will improve and your children will bring you joy. If you are awaiting some news, rest assured that everything will turn out well.

15 Ch'ien

Symbolizes holding one's tongue

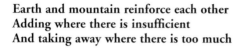

Earth and mountain reinforce each other
Adding where there is insufficient
And taking away where there is too much

This hexagram describes a successful and modest person whose inner wealth is hidden and not visible to the eye. The depths of his/her value lie in the shadow of the high mountain, so here the high and low complement each other. When it is time to embark on a venture, how can there be anything but success?

According to the I Ching, Ken, the mountain, placed below is the youngest son, so here we see the mother with her youngest son, for Kun the mother is above. They are both symbolic of earth chi – an auspicious indication. Success and also a certain indulgence are indicated. The oracle says, 'To cross the great water is beneficial, for it brings good fortune.' Thus travel, a new venture, a change of profession, a move to another part of the country – all will bring good fortune. The hexagram suggests that as long as there is clarity and strength hidden inside a modest veneer, good fortune is all but assured.

The Elements

Kun above Ken signifies big earth sitting on small earth, the mother above the son. The elements signify complete accord, with one being the resource of the other. Earth energy doubled helps the strength of relationships – there is support and goodwill. If the elements turn negative, it can suggest competition. The nuclear trigrams are Chen above and Kan below – water below wood – an excellent productive combination.

The Moving Lines

Line 1 (at the bottom): Travelling and new responsibilities are indicated in equal measure by this line. Both lead to success. If you are asking about a new job offer note that your abilities are well recognized and appreciated. If you are asking about your love life it too is looking good. Good fortune awaits you.

Line 2: There is some good fortune and it does not matter what you do. However you respond you will attract good fortune, so stay cool and rejoice in it.

Line 3: Undertakings will be profitable and many opportunities for advancement will come your way. Be bold and grab them.

Line 4: This is a good time to consolidate and take stock, not to be seeking advancement or promotion. It is also not a good time to get married or to commit. Be patient and wait for better things to unfold.

Line 5: This line brings immense benefits and great success. You will attract the eye and patronage of some very influential people, but there is a need for absolute discretion. No matter how well you are doing and how happy you are feeling, refrain from telling the world about it. In this instance silence is golden, for it does lead to greater things. Spill the beans and you could watch your good fortune evaporate.

Line 6: Avoid remorse and definitely never live your life regretting some action or inaction. Learn from every miscalculation and weakness. Life comprises lots of lost opportunities, so just be alert to the next one. This line is telling you to develop greater awareness of your role within the cosmos. Develop your powers of observation.

16 Yu

Symbolizes eagerness to start

Thunder brings a sudden release of tension
Reflecting an enthusiasm that refreshes nature
The ancient kings offered music
In celebration of the Supreme Deity

This hexagram is the essence of enthusiasm and happiness. It suggests a time for new ventures, a change of job, travel – anything that catches your imagination. It will be beneficial to start a new business, climb a mountain, build a new house and so on. If you get this hexagram it encourages you to prepare and plan for the new project. The best time to begin the project is somewhere between winter and spring.

The Elements
Chen (wood) above Kun (earth) indicates a destructive situation. The nuclear trigrams indicate Li (fire) above Ken (earth), a productive relationship. While superficial indications are negative, the hidden essence of this hexagram is productive and positive.

The Moving Lines
Line 1 (at the bottom): Refrain from boasting about your triumphs and successes – they attract envy and jealousy. If you are on a roll and want confirmation of continued success, this line is telling you to curb your enthusiasm. Your good luck will continue. Those in the scholastic field will enjoy sudden recognition. College students are offered what they apply for, which may be a scholarship or admission to a coveted course.

Line 2: Retreat. This line offers an excellent positive prediction. You should proceed with what you asked about, be it a personal, professional or career matter. Decide to move quickly and without hesitation. You will enjoy success in what you do.

Line 3: Sudden setbacks to your plans will bring remorse and make you feel regretful. This appears to be an unstable time for you and luck is uncertain. But there is a dilemma, for to delay now could cause problems but to continue will also bring failure. In the circumstances the advice is to try and change direction.

Line 4: Great gains are forecast by this line. You will succeed in your job applications and in your search for financing. Your plans enjoy positive luck and, if you work with enthusiasm, you will have cause to celebrate.

Line 5: Initial obstacles will delay the start of your project. One problem after another occurs to give you headaches. It seems that your ventures and plans just cannot get started. What you need is the help of someone powerful – a benefactor or mentor. Activate the north-west of your office with metal energy.

Line 6: This line indicates a dangerous period, especially for those who may not have been totally honest. Corrupt practices will cause you to be found out, so disgrace and humiliation could follow. If you have been honest and sincere there is no ill luck.

17 Sui

Symbolizes obedient participation

The I Ching offers the image of thunder
Churning the waters of the lake
After much activity
The superior man knows how to recuperate

This hexagram indicates a young man wooing a pretty girl who is single and eligible. He is successful, but the trigram Tui above signifies sunset and the approach of the night. Beauty and attraction are impermanent – they fade with the light. If you receive this hexagram the oracle advises against new entanglements, as your feelings cannot last.

   This hexagram is also an encouragement to rest and recuperate. After work and activity, you need a break – otherwise there can be a tiredness of the spirit. The hexagram is also encouraging you to take time off from what you are doing. In the long run, it will bring you greater success.

The Elements
The primary trigrams indicate metal above and wood below and the relationship is destructive, suggesting that it is better to rest than to be active. The nuclear trigrams are Sun (wood) above Ken (earth) – also a potentially destructive pairing. The indications are certainly negative.

The Moving Lines
Line 1 (at the bottom): Good fortune comes again and again. You will be going through a period of increased social activity where invitations flood in. Everything seems to be easy. If you get this line it means you can sit back and enjoy a period of probably well-deserved good time.

Line 2: This line offers a negative prediction. It suggests that a young person will cause anguish and scandal. It is necessary to watch your behaviour and react carefully. When the situation is handled with sensitivity the misfortune will blow over, but otherwise the scandal will get bigger, bringing remorse.

Line 3: You are placed in a situation where you have to choose between two courses of action. Both will have problems. If the dilemma is too difficult opt for the choice of doing nothing.

Line 4: A powerful man/woman brings good fortune, saving you from ruin. From a time of troubles, suddenly

your luck has transformed and high position as well as recognition will come to you. If a single large butterfly visits you in your home or office this prediction is certain. Butterflies stand for transformation luck and the energy of change is powerful. If you see butterflies in the garden it is also a good sign.

Line 5: Honourable behaviour will bring you good fortune, attracting the kind of success you have been dreaming of. You will get your big break and the opportunity to do what you have always wanted to. There is also success in the immediate future.

Line 6: There is some danger for your reputation caused by envious people who are jealous of your good fortune. Be magnanimous and share your good fortune with others. If you demonstrate a generous disposition your good luck will increase even more.

18 Ku

Symbolizes inner turmoil

**When the land has been spoiled
And there is decay
The superior man stirs the people
His belief strengthens their spirit**

Here is a hexagram that indicates severe problems, when the situation has reached rock bottom; a time of emotional disease. The image here is of the wind blowing low, under the mountain, destroying the vegetation. Decay has set in due to the chi stagnating. At other levels of imagery, this hexagram also suggests an older woman being involved with a young man – the relationship has reached a level of unhappiness and they must part. In business this hexagram also indicates that misfortune has set in. The situations you find yourself in are indeed tough and difficult to redress.

This is a time when perseverance and a belief in your fate changing are needed. Emotions need to be repaired and businesses must be rebuilt. The hexagram implies there will be limited success in the rebuilding process. Plants grow once more when nurtured with water and care, but attitudes and emotions take a longer time to heal.

The Elements
Wood below earth indicates a negative destructive relationship. The nuclear trigrams are Chen (wood) above Tui (metal), also a destructive relationship. It seems the signs are negative both inner and outer. Things do not look promising for the immediate future.

The Moving Lines
Line 1 (at the bottom): This line advises you to look for help outside yourself. Ask your father and family for assistance and advice. There are difficulties and danger, but if your family helps you have a good chance to turn things around. If you are facing a dilemma it is also a good idea to look to your family for help.

Line 2: Hard work and perseverance are necessary for you to climb out of your current difficult time. It is unrealistic to expect things to immediately get better. In a relationship that has suffered decay you must work hard at repairing the damage, while at work you face an uphill climb to regain trust which has been lost.

Line 3: It is necessary to curb your ambitions and impatience. This line warns against acting on impulse. What looks good today may not be so tomorrow. Do not be fooled by illusions.

Line 4: This line indicates a period of difficulty when everything goes wrong. You cannot find what you are looking for, and life seems boring and meaningless, but if you are patient things will seem different once the season changes. Until then, however, you will have to put up with strong criticism and scolding. It is not so bad – scoldings are easier to bear than physical hardship, ill health or beatings.

Line 5: This line shows a good time for you. Your feelings of remorse will dissipate and it will be as if they never existed. A marriage is indicated. Students and managers will start afresh in new jobs and new careers. There is the promise of fast advancement, but you should also work hard. Do not allow good fortune to make you careless.

Line 6: This line also indicates a good period, but it is still not the right time to start anything new. Be patient. Use this period of good fortune to acquire new knowledge and learn new skills. Soon you will find what you are looking for.

19 Lin

Symbolizes different classes of people

Two powerful lines thrusting upward
Signify the coming of spring
The hibernation is over
Once again there is activity

Many meanings are indicated by this hexagram. First there is the image of the mother and the daughter, Kun above and Tui, the youngest daughter, below: here the suggestion is the daughter benefiting from the nurturing care and guidance of her mother. Kindness and experience are indicated and the image is positive.

The two yang lines thrusting up from the bottom signify growth and vitality, indicating good fortune and high aspirations for the coming months. The advice thus suggests that it is beneficial to continue with what one is doing. The oracle encourages the feeling of optimism but warns only that you be careful during the eighth month.

The Elements

The primary trigrams indicate earth above metal, an exhaustive relationship showing that success comes only with effort. The nuclear trigrams also have Kun (earth) above Chen (wood), a negative relationship. This would suggest that the coming months require determination and hard work if you are to have success.

The Moving Lines

Line 1 (at the bottom): There will be limited success at work and in your studies. But help is coming from a person of influence, so mentor luck is on the way.

Line 2: Excellent outcomes are indicated in all your undertakings. Especially good indications for those asking about their professional lives, be it a change of scene, a new posting or a new challenge. There is good reason to celebrate, because more than career success awaits. There are unexpected surprises.

Line 3: This is a particularly boring time. It appears that there is little evidence of success luck in what you are contemplating. The oracle suggests that you look elsewhere for stimulation. If things have been bad and you are feeling depressed, consider taking up meditation, for introspection seems to be more beneficial than activity at the moment. In time the future will look rosier.

Line 4: Harmonious relationships bring good cheer and happiness. Opportunities abound for those whose enthusiasm for life leads them to investigate different options. Taking up any of these will bring satisfaction.

Line 5: This is the line that promises the greatest good fortune. It seems that the prospects for your choices are all excellent. Your plans have a very high chance of success and you will find satisfaction in what you decide to do. Everything will run smoothly and wherever obstacles appear you will have no problems overcoming them. But stay on track and try not to get easily distracted.

Line 6: Great good fortune is indicated for you if you get this changing line. All endeavours and ideas bear the imprint of success. You have good reason to rejoice. It is necessary only to remind you that you cannot do everything, so think through what you want to do carefully, whether the decision concerns your personal or professional life. Remember, the key to success is commitment and it is vital that you remain focused. When you try to do too many things success luck dissipates.

20 Kuan

Symbolizes looking, seeing, confronting

The wind blows over the earth
Moving far and wide
Gently observing the people and the land
Even as the grass bends
To the easy grace of its power

This hexagram signifies dust being blown by the wind. It settles in a faraway mountain. The image is of the width and breadth of the land, of the distances covered by the wind and of the height of the mountains. The hexagram suggests that success must be found elsewhere, in another part of the country or even abroad; there is also a suggestion of contemplation, of being lord of all you survey. It advises taking the macro view, like a bird flying high above the land and seeing a vision that is broad and all-encompassing.

When we equate the power of the wind to that of a person, it suggests someone of great charisma. Such a person is surely a ruler, a king, a leader of mankind. This hexagram is excellent for anyone contemplating a profession in the political arena, for it predicts an evolution of personality that will impress people so profoundly there will be huge success. They will be swayed by his words in the same way that the wind sways the grass. But such a path is not without its dangers. There will be sacrifices to come and sincerity of motivation is called for. The wind blowing signifies the need to observe and to learn.

The Elements

Sun (wood) is above Kun (earth), a destructive relationship. The nuclear trigrams, however, indicate Ken above Kun (earth over earth), suggesting a doubling of the matriarchal force. The core essence of this hexagram suggests that there is treasure hidden within the mountain if only you know how to access and mine for it.

The Moving Lines

Line 1 (at the bottom): Your efforts, however well planned and executed, will not bear fruit. Betrayals will shock you and opportunities for advancement will dry up. This line indicates a very difficult time indeed. The higher you are in your career, the harder you will fall. Alas, you must be prepared for humiliation.

Line 2: A good prediction for women, who will advance easily in their goals. But for men the outcome of what they are asking will be both trying and frustrating.

Line 3: This line suggests a time of ups and downs. There is a need for caution and it is important not to get carried away with easy and small successes. There could be a sudden disaster, so it is good to be wary and alert.

Line 4: Business or professional travel will bring success. Going overseas is most beneficial. Those moving abroad, crossing the great waters, to a new assignment or to take up a course at a foreign university will find fantastic success that brings widespread recognition.

Line 5: The prediction for this line is very good. Success is indicated in all you undertake, although the further away you stay from home the better your achievements. Illness will see recovery and family life is excellent.

Line 6: This line indicates a period of contemplation of the self as well as of the immediate environment. Take time off to look deep within yourself, allowing the inner wisdom to surface. It does not have to be for a long period – perhaps weekends of contemplation in a place far away from home would be most beneficial.

21 Shih Ho

Symbolizes wrathful

**It is through adherence to laws
That society becomes civilized**

This hexagram describes obstacles, quarrels and conflicting attitudes. It requires a courageous man to directly confront the conflicting parties and come up with solutions. The lines of the hexagram are shaped like a mouth which cannot close because it is filled with food. Only by biting through the food can the mouth close and the teeth come together to provide nourishment. This indicates directly coping with a problem or problems. It also suggests the need for courage and compromise. The bottom three lines indicate tough times at the start, but there is a breakthrough and then there is good fortune ahead. For marriage this hexagram indicates that someone will come between the husband and the wife or two lovers. The oracle advises confronting the problem to resolve it successfully.

The Elements
Li above signifies fire while the trigram below is Chen signifying wood. Here wood fuels the fire signifying a situation of production. Wood enhances the fire element bringing strong yang energy which when positive means strength and when weak signifies fire getting too hot. Fire brings fame and recognition. The nuclear trigrams symbolize Kan (water) above Ken (earth) – danger.

The Moving Lines
Line 1 (at the bottom): It is necessary to be cautious in whatever you are thinking of doing to avoid the danger of a personal disaster. Try to delay whatever you are pursuing. At work stay low key and do not be too noisy.

Line 2: There are gossip, injury to you, sickness and frustration. Someone will slander you and cause you difficulties. If you are working and the problem is at the office, take some leave and go on holiday. Let time take care of the frustrations in your life. If you have to go to the office, invest in a coin amulet and place the image of a rooster on your desk (such images are said to be excellent at 'pecking away at troublemakers'). A dragon tortoise (a creature with the head of a dragon and body of a tortoise) is also good protection. Do not overdo things, though, as there is no need.

Line 3: You can succeed but will have to work hard to do so. Even small triumphs are difficult. There is also some danger to your well-being and your financial position, so be careful. This is not a good time to expand or invest in new ventures. In relationships it is better to socialize with old friends than new.

Line 4: At last there is a breakthrough. This line spells good fortune, bringing with it the promise of upward mobility, high honours and recognition, success in relationships and reconciliation in old quarrels. The profits begin to roll in.

Line 5: There is further good fortune. Line 5 is always powerful and in this case it promises 'gold at the doorstep'. Sickness sees recovery, while lost objects will be found. What has been taken from you will also be returned.

Line 6: This final line spells misfortune and humiliation. There is a feeling of insecurity caused by a string of troubles and problems. The best thing to do is to backtrack.

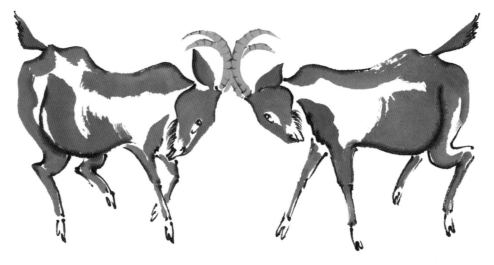

22 Pi

Symbolizes grace and beauty

Fire at the base of the mountain
Suggests a slow and gentle shining
Grace and beauty are full of charm
They appeal even more when there is substance

Success is indicated by this hexagram whose image is of fire burning at the base of the mountain. The image is auspicious and the elements are in sync, since fire produces earth. The lines also suggest the sun is shining brightly on the mountain, lighting up plants, flowers and trees. The trigrams represent a handsome couple as well, vivacious and glamorous and admired from afar. They seem elegant and look happy. So all the indications suggest material and physical success.

The Elements

Both the primary and nuclear trigrams are productive. The outer trigrams have fire producing earth, while the inner trigrams have water producing wood. So the good fortune is more than skin deep. There is cause for rejoicing.

The Moving Lines

Line 1 (at the bottom): It seems that your life is looking good and you have the basic requirements in place. All that is needed now is hard work and motivation. This line favours those of you entering your nesting period – starting a family, having a baby.

Line 2: This line indicates that something fresh and new is opening up for you very soon. There is the luck of a new opportunity coming. Be alert so you can spot it when it happens. Someone unexpected will help you, maybe even someone you already know but have not noticed before.

Line 3: Success comes easily for you if you get this line. There is no need to worry, even when things seem a little out of kilter. Friends help you, family is supportive and work colleagues think well of you. If you are feeling depressed it is all in your mind. Change your attitude and you will see things in a different light.

Line 4: Even in the midst of sadness there will be cause to rejoice. Early opposition will thus give rise to harmony and happiness. A white horse brings good fortune, so an image of a white horse, whether in a painting, on TV or in a book, signals the start of a period of good fortune.

Line 5: This line suggests that big success will be difficult to achieve but you will enjoy a series of small triumphs that build up through this good period. They will make you realize that both at work and in your relationships things are moving smoothly.

Line 6: This line indicates that you are seeing life with new eyes, appreciating the simple pleasures. You are discovering that there is more to life than just making money and this brings a great deal of satisfaction. Overall your life is blessed with good fortune.

23 Po
Symbolizes finality of death

The knife slashes against the plant
Decapitating it, removing branches and bark
Instantly killing what once was
A beautiful sentinel of the garden
So sad

This is truly a miserable hexagram, suggesting decay, death and the disintegration of things you hold dear. Here is a hexagram with a single yang line above and below all is yin weakness. The dark lines are threatening to overthrow the single white line, which suggests forces undermining you. In terms of trigrams, here Ken is sitting on Kun. Though they are both earth, it is earth placed in a way that seems most inauspicious. There is no solid support, nothing within. The hexagram indicates misfortunes in activity. It does not benefit to travel, to start anything or to give in to inferior people who would wish to harm you.

The best way to respond if you get this hexagram is to stay quiet and still. Like the mountain, stillness gives rise to contemplation and is also in rhythm with the attributes of the hexagram. If you are being confronted by someone, the best response is to submit. This is not the time to be a hero. It is not cowardice that makes you surrender but wisdom that encourages you to survive to fight another day.

The Elements
All four trigrams, primary and nuclear, are earth. There is therefore an excess – in other words, there is too much darkness. This does not appear auspicious.

The Moving Lines
Line 1 (at the bottom): There is discord among your relatives or partners. Alas, all this quarrelling and friction can only lead to disintegration and decay – and it could indeed spell the end of your collaboration. It seems unfavourable to do anything and indeed there is nothing you can do except to stay quiet and go with the flow.

Line 2: There is so much bad luck that anything that can go wrong will. Plans go awry, people betray you,

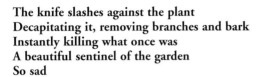

friends let you down, school results are worse than you expected and there is no success at work. Those in a career could even lose their jobs. If you get this line invest in some kind of coin or crystal amulet as they can be very effective in warding off bad chi.

Line 3: Everything falls apart. If you get this line note that friends will desert you when you most need them and colleagues will betray you. It is not a good time for relationships. Wear a crystal or better yet a gemstone that is suitable for you or with which you have an affinity. The earth energy will be able to hold off the bad effects of relationship woes.

Line 4: There is enormous danger if you get this line. The threat of lawsuits and bad luck causes difficulties to escalate suddenly. It is vital for you to check your office or home for the presence of quarrelsome stars if you are well versed in Feng Shui. If you are not, invest in a Happy Fat Buddha, who wears a red robe and is depicted carrying a gold ingot. This is the traditional cure that can overcome legal problems and hostile intentions. In the Western tradition perhaps displaying the image of Santa Claus might also work, since Santa does resemble the happiness Buddha.

Line 5: The power of line 5 comes to the rescue in this generally disastrous hexagram. If you get this line it indicates some success coming with the help of a woman. Women getting this line will also enjoy good fortune and success. This line is beneficial for scholars.

Line 6: The sixth line warns you to be very careful about keeping within the law. If you break the law, however trivial, you will be caught and then it will cause you a great deal of inconvenience. If you are law-abiding and honourable this line suggests that you will be able to overcome bad luck.

24 Fu

Symbolizes a turning back

Butterflies transform from humble worms
To become glorious beauties
Thunder rumbles from beneath the earth
Bringing positive change in the seventh month

This hexagram indicates that bad times have gone and luck has turned, so anyone getting it will see their fortunes transform and improve. The image is of a turning point, a transformation. Here the trigrams are Chen below and Kun above – and this reflects the natural order of things. The single yang line pushing upward signifies the sapling pushing through the earth. It will soon become a big tree – it only takes seven months. What is suggested here is a person whose energy has been made strong through recuperation. It can be interpreted also as health returning after recovery, relationships repairing after estrangement and life getting better after a time of drought. In these early stages, it is important to treat everyone with tender loving care. It is good to be sensitive and nurturing, as this will create the cause for an ultimate flowering of good luck.

The Elements
Here again all the trigrams are earth, but now the single yang line is below. This means their positioning reflects the course of nature and is thus auspicious.

The Moving Lines
Line 1 (at the bottom): There is great good fortune. Thunder in the earth announces a revival of fortunes. Profits return, grades are excellent, romance flourishes and relationships bring happiness. If you get this line it is strengthened further if you also see a butterfly or if there is a loud noise brought about by thunder and lightning on the day you consult the oracle.

Line 2: This line suggests you might be caught in some kind of predicament or embarrassing situation. Do not worry, as you will be rescued. Those who are sick will get better and losses will be recovered.

Line 3: This line suggests changing times. There is success coming to you, but it is slow. Do not fret unduly when you make mistakes or negative things happen to you. It benefits

workshops that will help you to grow as a person. This will benefit your family and give you greater confidence in what you do.

Line 5: Great success is indicated at work and your career takes off. There is, however, the danger of a personal tragedy occurring. Brace yourself. It will not be so hard that you cannot bear it, but you might want to make a generous donation to charity and dedicate it to the good health of your family and relatives. This can sometimes delay the occurrence of the tragedy.

Line 6: This seems like a time of danger and the indications are that if you engage in competition with anyone you will be defeated. So it is advisable to stay low key and walk away from provocation.

25 Wu Wang

Symbolizes innocence

Struggling against the blue sky
Such foolishness
Is surely futile

This hexagram signifies the natural order of things. Chien, the heavenly trigram, is above, while the trigram of movement, Chen, is below. There is the suggestion of innocence, of mankind being intrinsically good. The focus seems to be on the divine spirit within mankind. Thus heaven rewards those who persevere and those whose motivation and actions reflect the righteousness of the divine. At a practical level this hexagram advocates adapting to circumstances and advises against opposing the natural laws of right and wrong. It also advocates that children should obey their father and that subjects should listen to their ruler. There is a strong Confucian influence in the interpretation of this hexagram in that the natural order seems to stress the superiority of the state and of the family elders.

The Elements

Here the primary trigrams are metal above wood, a destructive relationship that reflects father and son. As long as the son obeys the father there is no problem. In the nuclear trigrams Sun is above Ken, so wood is resting on earth, once again indicating a destructive relationship. Here the eldest daughter controls the youngest son.

The Moving Lines

Line 1 (at the bottom): This line indicates that everyone benefits. There is good fortune when all parties cultivate virtuous behaviour and together persevere towards a common goal.

Line 2: This line is awesome. It predicts fame, money and property to the person who receives it, and also promotion and scholastic excellence. Those in business will enjoy very good profits, while those in relationships will receive good news. This is a very auspicious line.

Line 3: This line indicates good fortune for those in business and involved with commercial activities but is not as good for scholars or lovers. Those who are ill also need time to recover.

Line 4: There is good luck for everyone – business people, career managers, scholars and those who are thinking through their love relationships. Projects will succeed and no one will lose money.

Line 5: This powerful line brings success for your plans, so you can proceed with confidence. You can count on significant improvements to the health of your loved ones and also on your colleagues supporting you.

Line 6: If you do not have the talent to do your work adequately you will suffer misfortune. This is a warning line which suggests you spend time and effort improving yourself. If you are still in school or at college this line is advising you to study more seriously.

26 Ta Ch'u

Symbolizes big involvement

Taming the great requires great perseverance
It benefits to eat outside the home
It benefits to cross the great waters
Thus the superior man readies himself

This hexagram predicts a successful and very bright future, even hinting at certain greatness of attainments, perhaps something beyond your imagination at present. Here the image is of heaven within the mountain, suggesting there are hidden depths to your good fortune. And indeed, when you read the texts of the I Ching it speaks of 'hidden treasures' and also of 'the taming power of the great'. You should therefore be very excited if you obtain this hexagram in answer to a question about your future, especially in relation to your professional work or your business.

Since there is such a strong hint of success in the future, it should also give you the confidence to be bold and courageous in whatever you are planning to do. If you are in business and are about to launch a big project, move ahead without hesitation, for it seems that luck is on your side and the gods are behind you.

The Elements

Metal is below earth, an exhaustive and productive relationship. It is heaven that is exhausting the mountain, suggesting that success in mining the treasures of the mountain will tire you but you should persevere. In the nuclear trigrams Tui is below Chen (metal below wood), a destructive relationship. It could suggest the effort it will take to reach your goal may well kill you, so it is important to take a deep breath and not overtax yourself.

The Moving Lines

Line 1 (at the bottom): In the face of danger you should pause and wait. This line suggests that you take a few steps backwards, as obstacles will make an appearance.

Line 2: Watch your health and take it easy because you may be working too hard. If your health suffers, all the success in the world is of no value, so do look after yourself. It is also unfair on your loved ones if you fall ill.

Line 3: This is a time to advance and seize the initiative. Look out for new opportunities and avenues of growth and you will succeed. Creativity will be rewarded and hard work will bring huge returns.

Line 4: Unrestrained success is indicated by this line. Great good fortune is coming and you should be ready to receive many things. This line indicates that luck is on your side and confirms that you are on the right path.

Line 5: This line suggests that you will be offered a high position or an appointment you simply cannot refuse. You must accept it with confidence, for it will open amazing opportunities and lead to even greater success and happiness.

Line 6: Heaven is solidly behind you and success comes in every aspect of your life. You can be sure that nothing will hold you back. Rise to the occasion and to the challenges that will confront you but stay grounded. Success tastes sweet when accompanied by a genuine sense of gratitude and humility.

27 I

Symbolizes nourishment

**There is a need to be careful with one's words
When one is eating and drinking
Or simply using one's mouth**

The image of this hexagram is of an open jaw chewing food, giving nourishment to the body. The mouth gives voice to our inner thoughts and it is necessary to watch what we allow it to say. This is because the mouth represents speech and idle chatter can often be the cause of big problems.

If you get this hexagram the oracle offers encouragement, for there is success implied in the image of nourishment. But the oracle also warns against taking care of the right people. To succeed in this world, it is necessary to differentiate between the important and the unimportant, as well as to differentiate between the inferior and the superior. It is vital to 'cultivate the superior parts of nature'.

The Elements
Ken (earth) is above Chen (wood), which is a destructive relationship that does not seem to augur well for the recipient for this hexagram. You need to be careful. The nuclear trigrams are all earth and in this case this seems to be auspicious, indicating that the core of the hexagram has potential for great good fortune when the advice of the I Ching is followed.

The Moving Lines
Line 1 (at the bottom): This line indicates a severe repercussion from slanderous words spoken in a careless moment. The arrogance of speech leads to slander, which in turn leads to grave misfortune. If you get this line be very careful and make a special effort to watch your speech.

Line 2: This line offers the answer to your question – and it says that whatever you are asking about will not succeed. This is a time to be very alert.

Line 3: Misconduct is strongly predicted. The oracle warns strenuously against arrogance, dishonesty and slander. It would do well for you to look inwards and see if there is room for improvement.

Line 4: The image is of a hungry man hunting earnestly for food. There is a sense of desperation but there is good news, for he will be successful. No blame is assigned.

Line 5: Travel by ship or plane can be disastrous. This is a warning line and you should take heed. If you postpone or cancel your travel plans, there will be good fortune.

Line 6: Nourishment is found in abundance. This line indicates great success and it benefits to continue. Jobs are found, grades are excellent and the sick recover. There is good news all round.

28 Ta Kuo

Symbolizes great excess

The lake rises above the trees
Flooding the surrounding landscape
Bringing disaster or opportunity
When it comes depends on you

This hexagram presents an image of trees under water, and the hexagram itself shows four strong lines held together by two weak lines. This can mean several things. That your ambitions surpass your capabilities; that you have perhaps over-expanded your business; that you are living beyond your means; that your heart is breaking; that things are near to collapse and that quick and smart action is called for.

The hexagram suggests a special moment in time when things can go either way. Whether the situation leads to disaster or good fortune depends on how it is perceived, positively or negatively. While appearances indicate a dangerous overflow – even the trees are under water – if there is a superior response conditions can still lead to great success. The moment calls for genuine talent and is really quite significant, though it may not appear so. Meanwhile, it might be timely to remember that situations of great excess are usually temporary.

The Elements

Tui (metal) is above Sun (wood), so the relationship is destructive, indicating a negative situation. The nuclear trigrams are both Chien, which suggests metal on metal – a situation of continued hardness. But it is positive and can be read as holding the promise of a spectacular transformation into something good.

The Moving Lines

Line 1 (at the bottom): The oracle advises a slow and steady approach to whatever it is you are asking about. There seems to be plenty of time for you to find your levels of comfort. If you rush there could be obstacles. It is better to gain experience.

Line 2: This line indicates that you will have success in romantic matters, even though the woman seems older (or more mature) than the man. But if yours is a clandestine affair the future does not look good.

Line 3: There is misfortune on the cards. This line is suggesting that you might crack under pressure, so it is better to put some space between you and whatever is troubling you. Take a holiday or do something different to distract yourself, otherwise you could suffer humiliation and even get seriously ill.

Line 4: Good fortune comes with compromise. Take a soft approach. Give in to others and try to be less stubborn and dogmatic. This line indicates good luck in construction activity, so this may be a auspicious time to make renovations or build a new house. In careers there are promotion possibilities. Managers can advance.

Line 5: An older woman causes problems in your life. You must make some effort to dilute her influence, otherwise the situation can go from bad to worse. It will not be easy, as there appear to be some obstacles, but you must make the effort to set your house in order.

Line 6: This line indicates that there could be a sad event. Misfortune strikes where you are most vulnerable. Please wear a personal amulet for protection.

29 Kan

Symbolizes the Abysmal

Water moves in a continuous flow
Filling every crater and hole
The superior man follows and finds good fortune

The water trigram doubled spells grave danger. The Abysmal is suggesting situations that descend into a spiral of horrible happenings and dreadful situations. Water always suggests a valley, a hole, a depression that can fill and overflow. There is an inevitability about continuously flowing water, which can consume all in its path, the good as well as the bad.

Therefore this hexagram indicates a situation where larger forces take charge of your situation and it is probably easier to flow with these. In daily life when you find yourself swept along by a tide of opinion or a development over which you have no control, the best way to respond is to keep your counsel, stick to your principles and ride along. Water is a very powerful force. It is impossible to fight, especially when it overflows. You will have to wait until the flow slows down to a gentle trickle before taking action. Let the lines guide you on the best course to take. Water generally brings wealth, but when there is too much water it can be dangerous.

The Elements

The primary trigrams are both water, while the nuclear trigrams are Ken (earth) above Chen (wood), so, sadly, the relationship is not promising.

The Moving Lines

Line 1 (at the bottom): This line suggests misfortune that arises from the consumption of alcohol. Excessive drinking causes the mind to lose its clarity and can lead one into situations of danger. You should take this warning seriously. It is also warning you about friends who drink excessively. At work and in school there is danger of demotion and severe reprimands.

Line 2: This is a time to put your ambitions on the back burner. If you have just been offered a new job or are contemplating moving to a new position the oracle is advising against it. There will be tears and heartbreak. Best to keep a low profile.

Line 3: Great difficulties and conflicts mar your judgment. You must take a deep breath and prepare to be tough. You are facing a situation of some danger and this is not a time to be weak. Even the most simple situation can quickly deteriorate. Do not act in haste but be prepared to stand firm.

Line 4: This line suggests it is a good time to get married and to socialize. It is not a time for serious work or professional changes or relocations. There are, however, some small successes.

Line 5: The water is now under control and as a result it brings good fortune. The danger has receded and the worst is over. Opportunities are now within reach and it is a good time to be on the lookout.

Line 6: This line suggests really bad vibes. There are grave misfortunes ahead. Avoid entanglements at all costs. Pray if you are able to.

30 Li

Symbolizes clinging

The bright fire rises
Radiating light beams above
When you reach upward how can you fail?

The hexagram of double fire signifies bright sunlight, which indicates a moment of happiness. Fire needs continued nourishment if it is to stay bright. It requires fuel and nurturing, otherwise it dies. Fire must also be stable, otherwise it can be explosive and dangerous. When fire is under control it suggests fabulous good fortune. This is a hexagram that suggests a woman who is bright, clever and successful, someone who is beautiful both inside and out. She and all she encounters have the promise of lighting up the four corners of the world.

If you get this hexagram you should consider moving ahead with passion. If you are a young courting couple, this hexagram indicates marriage; if you are asking about your corporate affairs it urges you to expand. This is the time when opportunity knocks and you must take advantage. Fire generally brings success and recognition, but when there is too much it can be dangerous.

The Elements

The primary trigrams are both fire, while the nuclear trigrams have Tui (metal) above Sun (wood), so the relationship suggests inner danger. You also need to be careful, because too much fire outside could be destructive in the end.

The Moving Lines

Line 1 (at the bottom): This line urges you to proceed with caution, otherwise you might get burnt by your enthusiasm and passion. It can be a confusing and contradictory time when the signals you get from people seem incoherent.

Line 2: Sunlight represents great good fortune because it shines brightly, bringing a day with fine weather. The sun also nourishes. Profits are thus on the increase and your relationships are on an even keel.

Line 3: The sun has set and it is now twilight – not a good time. It seems that your question relates to something that is on the decline unless you re-energize it.

Line 4: This line reflects the danger of double fire – a fiery temper accompanied by insolence and arrogance. Volatile moods and anger do you no good at all. They lead only to conflict that in turn leads to unhappiness all round. Try to stay in control of your moods and feelings.

Line 5: This line suggests a period of mourning, but good fortune is just around the corner – perhaps the fire is cleansing. But do not expect too much, for the successes and triumphs stay small.

Line 6: This line suggests a lucky period when success will be easy to come by, but the line also indicates that loneliness may overshadow all attainments on the career front. Material gains will seem a little hollow.

31 Hsien

Symbolizes something felt in the heart

To marry now
Brings love and devotion
The image is of a receptive bridegroom

This hexagram means attraction, stimulation and affection – feelings that have to do with the heart. The image of coming together is very strong. It suggests a bonding, a marriage, which may be between either a couple or two companies. Whatever form the bonding takes, the hexagram indicates it is auspicious and will bring happiness and satisfaction. The trigrams indicate a joyous young woman, Tui, and a happy young man, Ken, and they are in the right places above and below, following the natural order of things. This suggests good luck and indeed even the texts say 'to take a maiden for a wife brings good fortune'. There will be harmony and expansion after the bonding.

The lines of this hexagram, however, do suggest that the recommendation to bond is more potent when received as a predictive rather than a base hexagram.

The Elements

The primary trigrams indicate that there is a pairing of metal and earth, a productive relationship that suggests good fortune. The nuclear trigrams are Chien (metal) above Sun (wood), a destructive relationship. This suggests hidden problems caused by an older woman and also by a much older man.

The Moving Lines

Line 1 (at the bottom): Wait patiently and choose your time carefully before proceeding. This line indicates that things have a favourable outcome.

Line 2: Good fortune lies in inactivity. Transfers lead to misfortune. Those contemplating marriage are advised to investigate the feelings of others before proceeding. There could be some small opposition.

Line 3: This is a lukewarm line. It advises you to expect only average luck. There is stimulation but little attraction. Oh dear!

Line 4: There is minor success, as all parties seem lacking in enthusiasm. With greater determination on your part, remorse disappears and good fortune comes within reach. It is necessary to verbalize your feelings and inner thoughts.

Line 5: Strong opinions on all sides cause discord and spoil things for you. If you can, refrain from reacting or responding to others' attempts to upset you. Do not rise to the bait!

Line 6: You can look forward to some small triumphs but will have to watch out for frivolous talk. Too much gossip could lead to conflict. You should not listen to hearsay.

32 Heng

Symbolizes constancy

With the constant moon shining
The heart sails through life
Like a boat between two shores

This hexagram signifies a strong and enduring marriage; it predicts a happy time for lovers. For those thinking about their careers, it is a time of high achievement; those with businesses can look forward to fat profits. Those in difficulties will find release from their entanglements. This hexagram urges perseverance for those engaged in projects or waiting for success. It is worth striving to attain excellence, for your efforts will be rewarded. This is because the hexagram predicts that everything will succeed. The thunder and wind of the trigrams are standing firm and do not change direction, despite their mobility, so there is duration. Things can last, and luck comes to those who have faith in themselves and a belief in what they do.

The Elements
Chen is above Sun (wood doubled), an auspicious sign. The nuclear trigrams are Tui above Chien (metal doubled), so the hidden meanings are also auspicious.

The Moving Lines
Line 1 (at the bottom): This line suggests that it is unnecessary to try too hard or be too insistent. Go with the flow, otherwise you could get caught up in words and then nothing benefits.

Line 2: Remorse disappears and stability will now be achieved. This line indicates that previous failures have been corrected. It is good from now on.

Line 3: Do not bring misfortune on yourself by offending people. There is never a good reason for doing this – it only feeds your ego. Better to stay silent when you feel like retaliating or succumbing to anger. In this instance, offending anyone leads to your own downfall, so do make the effort.

Line 4: You are in a difficult situation. You need to improve your present position before thinking of expanding, as there is a real risk of loss of money and profits. The opportunity cost will be even higher.

Line 5: For women this line indicates a successful time, but for men the opposite is true.

Line 6: Aim for modest successes and modest growth. This is a tough time for you and whatever you do will not have spectacular results.

33 Tun

Symbolizes running away

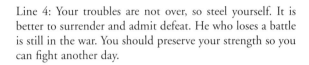

**The mountain rises up to the heavens
But heaven stays out of reach
Surely this suggests a lofty indifference**

This hexagram advocates retreat and withdrawal. It is saying that what you are asking for is like asking for the moon – out of your league and out of your reach. At a practical level it suggests a compromise and avoiding direct confrontation in anything. There is simply no chance of success. Like the hermit in the mountain, go back into your cave and contemplate your position.

For those in business this hexagram advises closing down and cutting losses. It is not a good time to continue as the outlook is bad. Also it is not a good time to start a new venture, diversify or expand.

The Elements
The primary trigrams indicate metal above earth, a productive relationship, while the nuclear trigrams are Chien (metal) above Sun (wood), which is destructive, so here is something that appears good outside but hidden dangers lurk.

The Moving Lines
Line 1 (at the bottom): Retreat. There is danger and you should avoid further entanglements in situations of conflict. This is because you have no chance of winning. You simply cannot prevail, so be warned.

Line 2: You can continue to expect contentious behaviour from friends and associates, but do not respond. There is benefit in keeping silent.

Line 3: Good fortune comes only if you can withdraw without entanglements. But watch out for hidden dangers.

Line 4: Your troubles are not over, so steel yourself. It is better to surrender and admit defeat. He who loses a battle is still in the war. You should preserve your strength so you can fight another day.

Line 5: You are blessed with good fortune indeed and your luck continues to get better. But it does so in small doses – nothing big or spectacular.

Line 6: Everything is beneficial. Material gains are forthcoming and business can flourish, but working people experience problems.

34 Ta Chuang

Symbolizes great wisdom

**The power from within is brought to life
And heaven signals its awakening
Movement and activity bring forth yang chi
Perseverance furthers**

The image of this hexagram is thunder in the sky, which signifies force and speed within human comprehension, as well as amazing yang power. The trigrams are Chien and Chen, a powerful combination that suggests the unleashing of great force: like a strong horse galloping in a burst of speed, or a young person's enthusiasm and passion. It is this that will capture success. The oracle only urges you to temper force with wisdom, to mix patience with your zeal, and then there will be success. But it does encourage you to proceed, for 'it benefits to continue'.

The Elements
Here the primary trigrams have wood above metal, which is potentially a destructive relationship, so outward danger is indicated. The nuclear trigrams are Tui above Chien (metal doubled), which reveals the hidden promise of finding gold – very auspicious indeed.

The Moving Lines
Line 1 (at the bottom): This line says now is a time when hasty action leads to remorse, so temper your haste and impatience because the line suggests you are not yet ready to begin.

Line 2: Persistence has its virtues and in your case it brings benefits. There is good fortune and you can achieve your objective, so proceed with confidence.

Line 3: Be cautious. This line is indicating hidden conflicts, which are about to be revealed. There is potential for disaster lurking around the corner. If you get a line like this the oracle is simply alerting you to the possibility that you might have secret enemies or that something unfortunate is about to occur. It is a good idea to wear some kind of amulet.

Line 4: A very good time to act. An excellent line to get, it says that if you yield to the pressures being placed on you, you will succeed beyond your wildest dreams. Also, if you observe auspicious images today, especially images of celestial creatures (dragons, phoenixes, etc.), fish or birds, they bring good news and opportunities. The only thing to remember is to stay 'cool' – take one day at a time.

Line 5: This line is indicating an unlucky time and there is a higher chance of failure than success. There will be a fair number of obstacles.

Line 6: Your problem will be your terrible arrogance and temper. This is already an explosive hexagram, and this line is even more so. There really can be disaster if you let your anger manage you instead of the other way around, so make an effort to calm your mind and your attitude. Take deep breaths each time you feel the fire rising.

35 Chin

Symbolizes meeting the great man

**There is progress when one meets the great man
And enhances one's virtues
For then the powerful prince
Invites you to eat at his table**

This is a superior hexagram, indicating upward mobility of substance. Now is a time for new beginnings, with very bright prospects for the future. If you are in business you will see it start to really take off, moving into a period of fast growth. You will achieve a high level of success. For career professionals there is promotion on the way. This hexagram is also favourable for marriage and moving into a new home.

But there is a need to work closely with others. A mood of cooperation should prevail among friends, colleagues and family. Much is indicated by this hexagram, but it is vital not to have discord, otherwise good fortune will simply dissipate immediately, turning into misfortune.

The image here is of the sun rising and bringing with it the bright light that transforms earth into a magnificent place. There is a purity in the sun's morning light and it reflects mankind's intrinsic goodness. For good fortune to continue, the purity of the light must not become clouded with inferior motives and negative actions. The I Ching constantly stresses the need for virtuous behaviour that is uncorrupt, for even the greatest good fortune can become altered by negative motivations.

The Elements

Li above signifies fire, while the trigram below is Kun signifying earth. Here fire creates earth, revealing a situation of production, which indicates enhancement. Fire enhances the earth element bringing excellent grounding energy. Earth always signifies nurturing. The nuclear trigrams symbolize Kan (water) above Ken (earth) a situation of danger.

The Moving Lines

Line 1 (at the bottom): There are obstacles that are blocking your path, but with hard work you can have them removed. Persistence is the order of the day and there is no reason why you cannot stay on course.

Line 2: You can expect to get unexpected help from your wife, mother, mother-in-law or aunt. An older woman extends a hand of friendship. It is a sincere gesture that can lead to great success. Initially, though, it may not seem so.

Line 3: You are blessed with many good friends and they help you very much to realize what you desire. This line is encouraging you to look to your immediate circle of friends for support and help. You will not be disappointed.

Line 4: There seem to be too many conflicts in your life right now, together with a lot of noisy disagreements. Regardless of the sudden upswing in your popularity, you must stay centred and grounded and not become big-headed, despite small successes.

Line 5: This line offers a reprieve, for it suggests something positive is coming. Remorse vanishes and everything will be as successful as you have planned. Things move along smoothly. Misunderstandings get cleared up. Sickness is cured and plans succeed. Big profits are also possible if you encounter a positive sign today – such as a significant phone call, or meeting an old friend unexpectedly.

Line 6: Incomes increase with this line. It is an especially good line for students, as it foretells spectacular success ahead. For those about to enter the job market, consider non-traditional areas of work or business. Taking some risks will bring you gains and no blame will be attached to any of your decisions. So go for it.

36 Ming I

Symbolizes a darkening

**Here the fire is hidden deep inside the earth
There is a darkening of the light
During times of troubles
The superior man strengthens his resolve
And goes bravely forward**

So much darkness is indicated by this hexagram that it seems to suggest there is evil everywhere. It can also indicate the night-time, when everyone and everything is asleep. At moments like this it is easy to surrender to the inevitability of bad times, to give up and give in to the unfavourable circumstances, but the oracle advises otherwise.

There is still an inner light, which need not be put out. If you keep this inner light burning you will have the energy and ability to overcome even the greatest adversity. It is advisable during bad times to hide your inner light, and your determination and perseverance are sometimes best kept hidden. Why? Because there is danger and it benefits to be cautious and reserved. Otherwise the evil eye will focus on you, thereby multiplying your difficulties.

The Elements
Kun (earth) is above Li (fire), a productive relationship that suggests good fortune. The nuclear trigrams are Chen above Kan, also productive, and here it suggests growth, for water produces wood, making it grow. So the hidden meaning is also excellent.

The Moving Lines
Line 1 (at the bottom): This line suggests a mixture of good and bad possibilities. There are obstacles and difficulties suggested but also the promise of great honour and prestige coming to you. You must be discerning in your judgment. It is also good to be wary of situations – do not get duped too easily.

Line 2: This line indicates power coming to you after a period of dark times. Be prepared and hold steady.

Line 3: There is no need to rush. Consider that during adversity we can afford to take our time. Be extra careful. Check things through before making any decisions that may have longer-term implications.

Line 4: Success comes with the goodwill of others. Word of mouth helps you more than anything else, so give others their due. Also watch your behaviour and responses to those who want to offer advice and help. Adopt a humble demeanour. This line also suggests a transfer to another location. A new job or assignment is successful for you, so when opportunity knocks do not miss it.

Line 5: Success can only be achieved in a foreign land, far from home. If you also discern signs of travel, or you start doodling cars and ships, this is a sign that your inner wisdom is encouraging you to consider living in another place. This means moving from your present home.

Line 6: Early triumphs give way to obstacles. Do not be indifferent or unconcerned. Apathy brings misfortune and losses. Stay alert to developments that take place around you. Make time for others.

37 Chia Jen

Symbolizes the family type

The matriarch strengthens the family
Wind from the fire
Symbolizes the family

This hexagram places emphasis on the family, advising that we should give it precedence above many things when we contemplate our options and choices. The I Ching always predicts happiness for those who give their family priority. Thus this hexagram is foretelling a happy outcome for those who are planning to get married, or to start/expand their family. If you are thinking of adoption, getting this hexagram predicts a happy outcome.

At another level this hexagram also focuses on the role of the matriarch. The mother holds the family together; without her it could well disintegrate. The hexagram is therefore suggesting that she should be taken into account in any decision you make.

The Elements
Sun (wood) is above Li (fire), an exhaustive relationship. The nuclear trigrams are Li (fire) above Kan (water), a conflicting relationship which does not augur well for the family.

The Moving Lines
Line 1 (at the bottom): You can expect success, and any forthcoming marriage will be auspicious, benefiting both families. For bridegrooms, please note that your wife will bring you luck, so honour and spoil her. You will notice that after marriage your fortune gets better and better.

Line 2: Success and increase of the family wealth are indicated. If you obtain this line you are on the right path and your actions are beneficial. For those still at college, applications for scholarships will be successful.

Line 3: Goodwill towards each other benefits everyone. This line stresses the importance of being sensible in your approach to your work and your relationships. Make a special effort to be civil to colleagues.

Line 4: Great good fortune is offered by this line. Income and wealth can be increased and popularity soars. This is an auspicious line – one that promises much. But you have to work at the opportunities that come your way. Good luck does not just happen.

Line 5: Patronage from men of power and influence brings wealth and good fortune. This means there is a great deal of mentor luck in your life right now. Be alert to the possibility that you might be singled out for a particular assignment. It represents a good opportunity.

Line 6: Sincerity and dignity bring good fortune. Your reputation will soon reach great heights, bringing you prestige and the respect of many people. Fill the south corner of your home with bright lights, as this will enhance the affinity of this luck. Those whose career puts them in the public eye will benefit from this line.

38 Kuei

Symbolizes opposition

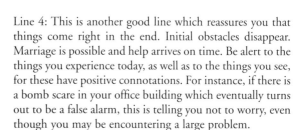

**Strange signs appear in the heavens and on earth
Are they our ancestors signalling their displeasure?**

This hexagram symbolizes the opposing energies of fire and water, for the trigrams indicate the lake above and the fire below. So the main theme of this hexagram revolves around the idea of conflicts, contradictions, opposition and hostility. Note that fire burns upward while water sinks, so the chi of the elements here moves in opposite directions.

But water also dampens fire, so it is not an auspicious hexagram, suggesting as it does the kind of energy which has a negative impact on situations. If you are about to sign a document, attend a meeting or conclude a deal, getting this as your predictive hexagram is telling you to delay. Think again about whether you really want to proceed or wait for a better time. It should serve as a dampener to your enthusiasm, because it predicts that there simply is no success possible. If this is the base hexagram, however, it is the lines that offer a more accurate picture.

The Elements
Li (fire) is above Tui (metal), but Tui also symbolizes a lake and hence water. The nuclear trigrams are Kan (water) above Li (fire), so the inner meaning is also full of conflict, perhaps of an even stronger variety, for here it is the trigrams themselves that are in disharmony.

The Moving Lines
Line 1 (at the bottom): Great discord at the beginning is indicated, but this will soon evaporate, to be replaced by goodwill and understanding. Progress to this stage will, however, take time, as initial suspicions must be allowed to give way to trust and reliance.

Line 2: This line indicates there can be good fortune if one is able to depend on friends and allies. Networking thus plays a large role in your eventual success, but there is little cause for anxiety since this is intrinsically a lucky line. Bosses also tend to be helpful in this instance.

Line 3: Small instances of annoying situations are indicated in the early stages but eventually your luck improves. There will also be some disappointment ahead, but in time this too should be overcome. This line is assuring you that, despite many small problems, things will ultimately be better.

Line 4: This is another good line which reassures you that things come right in the end. Initial obstacles disappear. Marriage is possible and help arrives on time. Be alert to the things you experience today, as well as to the things you see, for these have positive connotations. For instance, if there is a bomb scare in your office building which eventually turns out to be a false alarm, this is telling you not to worry, even though you may be encountering a large problem.

Line 5: Many benefits will arise from your various business undertakings so it is a good idea to keep working on them. Marriage is also indicated for those who are eligible and mergers bring good fortune. Promotion is also possible.

Line 6: Early losses are converted into profits at a later stage. This is a learning time for you and eventually confusion will clear up and ventures proceed smoothly. Learn to ignore frivolous opinions given with no thought and never allow your judgments to be clouded by tittle-tattle.

39 Chien

Symbolizes grave danger

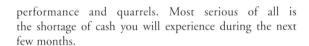

**Water unchecked and rising on the mountains
Will spill over causing loss and misery
A superior men ensures water is always kept under
    control**

One of the most dangerous hexagrams in the I Ching, this is a very strong warning that water is 'about to overflow'. The image is of water at the summit of a mountain, with a steep abyss ahead and the water rising. This hexagram also implies many obstacles blocking your life right now. One of the solutions given is to face the south-west, sit north-east and in this direction have a meeting with someone who can help you; or look towards the south-west for help. Another way is to form an alliance with friends who are in a similar situation and search for a good manager to assist you.

The oracle makes much of inner determination to overcome the adversity facing you. It advises against looking for scapegoats or assigning blame, which it describes as actions of 'the inferior man'. The best way to overcome obstacles is to be action-oriented. This hexagram suggests that water is the problem and excess water is often equated with excess greed. If that is the case here, it is a good idea to scale back on profits or expansion that is moving too fast.

If your question is personal and concerns marriage or love, the Oracle likewise warns against danger and obstacles. It is better to wait. Finally, if you are travelling, avoid flying towards the north-east. However, flying south-west will bring good fortune.

The Elements
Kan (water) is above Ken (earth), a destructive relationship which indicates danger. The nuclear trigrams are Li (fire) above Kan (water), which indicates a clash and a destructive relationship. This suggests that the hidden meaning of this hexagram is also most inauspicious.

The Moving Lines
Line 1 (at the bottom): This line advises you to remain inactive. If you are asked to relocate, politely decline unless it is to the south-west. Do not start a new venture or open a new shop. There will be obstacles hampering you all the way.

Line 2: This line indicates many obstacles, which will hit you in the form of illness, legal difficulties, poor staff performance and quarrels. Most serious of all is the shortage of cash you will experience during the next few months.

Line 3: If you are cautious, you will be able to prevent loss or injury. This is a good time for marriages, examinations and study, but not for making money. Financially there can even be serious loss, so it is best to stay pessimistic about the immediate outlook.

Line 4: Perseverance and hard work will bring their own rewards, but at work and in business there is a real danger of legal problems. It is better to stay aloof from other people's affairs and also to be as conciliatory as possible. This is not a time to engage in conflict.

Line 5: There will be very strong opposition to what you are thinking of doing. This can derail you and shake your confidence. But if you have the courage of your own convictions and proceed despite the setback, you will find yourself being supported by powerful people and influential friends. There is mentor luck coming round the corner. Be observant today and look out for auspicious signs. If you see anything that represents an auspicious aspect of life – for example, wealth objects or abundance items such as a lorry filled to the brim with products – this indicates that good fortune is definitely coming to you.

Line 6: This line advises you to identify and seek out a powerful mentor. Be confident, as luck is on your side. The line predicts that your talents and skill will find recognition with the right people. There will also be powerful support from a great man, but you must ask for it. Luck comes only to those who seek, and seek aggressively.

40 Hsieh

Symbolizes liberation

The ice melts and water flows freely again
If there is something to do
Doing it quickly brings good fortune

This is a happy and powerfully liberating hexagram. It announces a freedom from all obstructions. Shake off your shackles, because everything that has ever held you back is released. Internally and externally, you will now enjoy the freedom you have been craving for so long. The sense of liberation you feel is real. It makes you happy. The image is of ice melting during the springtime so that water can flow freely once more.

This can also be a metaphor to suggest that the obstacles holding you back are now released. Funds due to you that were so slow in coming are now paid; approval letters that held back work are now released. Many of your problems will be resolved.

The Elements
With wood above water, this is a productive relationship that spells good fortune. The nuclear trigrams are Kan (water) above Li (fire), a potentially clashing relationship, but both elements follow their natural flow, downward and upward respectively. This transforms water into steam, indicating hidden good fortune.

The Moving Lines
Line 1 (at the bottom): Success is suggested during this new period of growth. If you are single you will soon meet someone exciting and this could lead to marriage. There is good fortune indicated. Those already married could be blessed with a new baby. This line is most auspicious.

Line 2: This line advises you to continue with whatever you are doing – it can be your job or a new assignment or venture. There is great good fortune coming your way – almost like finding gold. Place symbolic wealth objects around your home, such as gold ingots and crystal 'wish-fulfilling jewels',

and also place the God of Wealth prominently in your living room, directly facing the main door. This will symbolically welcome in the wealth and is usually excellent for people who receive auspicious lines like this.

Line 3: If your luck seems to be bad now and life is one long and dreary journey, do not despair as your time will soon come. Although this is not a good line and it does not promise much, it is part of a good hexagram. Bide your time and soon things will change. Surround yourself with active and bright yang energy to cheer yourself up. Place a widely grinning Laughing Buddha on your table and let his happy image work some magic in your life.

Line 4: This line suggests that your associate is most trustworthy indeed, especially if he/she has been with you for some time. Be wary of friends you have just met. Do not judge people by their clothes; what is inside is far more important. Be observant of your surroundings each time you meet new friends and acquaintances. When something nice happens to you the signs are good, but if three negative things happen then the signs are bad.

Line 5: This line suggests a positive answer to all your questions. Illnesses get cured, what is lost can be found and even financial losses can be recouped. All-round good fortune is indicated and ventures are profitable. But do not gamble, as you are short on speculative luck.

Line 6: Careers take off beautifully if you obtain this line. This is due mainly to the affinity you have with your boss. Prestige, travel and money are indicated, but watch your health and make certain you get enough rest. When you are young you will not feel the strain on your body and mind, but unless you pace yourself correctly you could suffer from premature burnout. This is the most common ailment for those whose career luck starts to shine so dazzlingly.

41 Sun

Symbolizes loss

The lake at the base of the mountain
Suggests financial loss – on the outside
But a replenishment of riches within

This hexagram presents the image of decrease, suggesting financial loss or a contraction of business. It can also mean that you are experiencing severe monetary strain. It is important to watch your expenses and even initiate a cost-control exercise in your life, perhaps change your lifestyle.

When you receive a hexagram like this and it confirms your present state, you should not react negatively. The oracle is here to help you plan ahead by giving you advance warning of bad or tough times to come. In any case, the image of decrease is not always negative. Sometimes lessening the outward trappings of success is a good thing, because it forces you to take stock of your situation and ultimately your life. It could be the catalyst you need to make you see life from another perspective, becoming stronger in the process. Indeed this hexagram suggests that misfortune makes you into a better and deeper person.

A lake beside the mountain promises the potential for transformation of some sort to occur. If you live up to this advice there will be good fortune.

The Elements

Earth is above metal, an exhaustive relationship, while the nuclear trigrams are Kun (earth) above Chen (wood), a destructive relationship. So the hidden meaning of this hexagram is also inauspicious. There does not appear to be any respite in sight, so it is best to lie low.

The Moving Lines

Line 1 (at the bottom): The advice is that you should work out your budget carefully. Do not expand, but conserve your cash. Be careful not to over-commit. This is not a good time to be spending money.

Line 2: Maintain your normal routine and eat out less. Stay at home and look for more sedentary forms of activity. This line indicates that now is not a good time to change, so do not move and do not change your job or status.

Line 3: There is an active social period indicated. Friends rally round and offer more than moral support.

Line 4: Good fortune is very near to reaching you now so be prepared. Plans you had put on the back burner can now be revitalized.

Line 5: There are wonderful opportunities of good fortune indicated by this line. An unexpected windfall will surprise you and be very welcome indeed.

Line 6: Friends play a large part in helping you get on your feet again. This is a successful time when you can be more confident about moving forward.

42 I

Symbolizes increase

There is so much growth energy
It benefits to cross the great water
In perseverance there is good fortune

Increase is suggested by the lines of this hexagram, indicating an active and busy period in your life. Prosperity and expansion are indicated and this is also an excellent time for marriage, mergers and joint ventures to take place. It seems that even when others are negative about your plans, you should follow your own inclinations. Luck is with you and there is every reason to be confident. This luck will improve if your successes prompt a sense of generosity towards others.

For those involved in research and study, this hexagram suggests very meaningful progress which can even be described as some kind of breakthrough. If you are about to embark on a journey the signs are that it will be a significant one. In time what you sow during this period will bring you great prosperity.

The Elements
Here both primary trigrams are wood, while the nuclear trigrams are Ken above Kun (earth doubled), so two doubling effects make for a very auspicious relationship.

The Moving Lines
Line 1 (at the bottom): There is simply sublime good fortune. Everything in your life right now – your career, your family and your aspirations – move along smoothly. This is indeed a good period, so go ahead and do whatever it is that will bring you happiness.

Line 2: If you get this moving line it indicates magnificent good fortune. There is success in your endeavours and people seem to like you very much. You are in a period when friends increase and social life becomes most agreeable. If you are single you could meet someone exciting, but go slowly. Those already married will enjoy a phase of rediscovering each other.

Line 3: This is a line that suggests you might be experiencing some setbacks, but it should not worry you because even with a couple of hitches you will find success. There is promotion ahead and enhanced income. Those suffering the little arrows of jealous minds should learn to shrug off distasteful remarks. No amount of politicking will be able to shake your good fortune, but you should also be magnanimous – in victory it is always good to be big-hearted. The sight of a rooster image today will be particularly good. It means you will easily vanquish small enemies.

Line 4: This is a line of opportunity and a brilliant new opening is coming to you. At first it will seem too good to be true, but the advice of the oracle is to go for it. This sort of opening does not come often, and if you persevere and are genuine in your efforts, it will lead to other good things. Success is not difficult to attain.

Line 5: This line suggests that you will become an outstanding leader, so if you have just been asked to head some project or company, grab the chance. This will be a showcase for you, as you will gain recognition and achieve great honours. You will need to work hard and change your lifestyle, and career takes precedence in your life, encroaching more and more into your personal life, but you will be amply rewarded. This is a good line for those who are keen to forge ahead in their career.

Line 6: Jealousy and betrayal surround you at work. You will need to arm yourself against those who want to harm you. Your fears and premonitions are not without basis. Get a protective amulet and place a tortoise or a mountain painting behind you at work. This line suggests that the period of active politicking against you will blow over and you will experience victory, but watch your back at all times.

43 Kuai

Symbolizes determination

Success requires strength and determination
Fear not the bursting of a swollen river
The release of tension
Brings the breakthrough

Chien below Tui signifies a firm decision and it is this that enables the superior man to face all manner of obstacles. In life there will always be small-minded people whose idle chatter and active troublemaking cause problems. This hexagram describes a situation when suppressed anger and frustration at last break out. Where before there had been tension and covert politicking, now things are out in the open, so it is like a release.

The yin line suggests that this development is a good thing and will lead to positive results, which happen when you show your inherent strength and have the courage to be your own person. The successful leader is someone who is not afraid to spurn those who want to cause dissent. It is only by dealing decisively and fairly with the situation, and also by taking the needs and sensitivities of others into consideration, that you can succeed. The five yang lines indicate strength of character, which brings long-lasting triumphs and helps avoid the disaster and collapse that could so easily develop. Those who would be greedy will have victory snatched from them.

This hexagram's advice to be strong refers mainly to business and career. It does not apply to personal life and especially not to marriage or love affairs.

The Elements

Tui is above Chien (metal doubled), which suggests good fortune. The nuclear trigrams are Chien above and below, which is not merely metal doubled but suggests heaven doubled.

The Moving Lines

Line 1 (at the bottom): Determination can sometimes breed arrogance, which in turn leads to hostility. When this happens there will be cause for regret.

Line 2: If you suffer a sudden crisis of confidence try to overcome feelings of panic. The oracle is telling you that it is all in the mind and as long as you stay determined and optimistic your abilities will see you through, with events unfolding positively. If you woke up this morning with a sinking feeling and a sense of dread, it is a good idea to empower yourself with positive affirmations.

Line 3: This line warns against over-confidence and a dogmatic stubbornness which can derail all you have achieved in the past. Try a little humility when handling human problems within your organization.

Line 4: There will be some small setbacks that put a dent in your confidence level, but you should not allow these to hold you back. Success comes with resolve and you must develop an ability to hold firm.

Line 5: This line indicates difficulties by the dozen. These will discourage you, sapping your confidence, but stay resolute. The oracle is telling you to strengthen your resolve, because in the end you will succeed. If you see any of the symbols of victory – the victory horse, for instance – whether in your dreams, in a book or on a poster – this confirms that ultimately you will win through your difficulties. Do not allow manmade obstacles to stop you from staying strong.

Line 6: Misfortune is indicated by this line. It is better to withdraw than to proceed further. Return to the original plan if your difficulties become too severe.

44 Kou

Symbolizes an encounter

The wind blows under the sky
And bring about accidental meetings
Encountering a stranger
One sees new opportunities

This hexagram suggests that new situations arise without warning and the lines indicate a situation where a single female is surrounded by many suitors. She is bold and easy, and those who fall for her charms could well encounter heartbreak. Falling for her would seem like the act of an inferior person. The oracle advises you to stay aloof.

If you asked about your love life the yin line suggests a situation that is not conducive to permanent happiness. If you are a woman the image is of too many boyfriends; if you are a man the woman you admire and desire already has too many suitors.

If you asked about a job, the line suggests that what you have in mind may not be as good as you think and so it is better to look elsewhere.

The Elements
Chien (metal) is above Sun (wood), a destructive relationship that does not appear auspicious. The nuclear trigrams are Chien and Chien, so here there is a doubling of metal. The hidden meanings of the hexagram are auspicious – investigate further.

The Moving Lines
Line 1 (at the bottom): This line indicates legal problems – your chance encounters this month will bring you nothing but trouble. The oracle suggests that you should not get involved in other people's affairs and also stay aloof from blind dates or unexpected meetings. Do not allow surface attraction to someone of the opposite sex get you into trouble.

Line 2: You can expect benefits and favours from an unexpected source. However, your personal life suffers from a few setbacks. It is necessary to stay cool.

Line 3: There are many problems that are causing you to get stressed at work. This is quite an unhappy period for you, as disputes escalate quickly into major conflicts. This line does indicate success for those still engaged in studies, though.

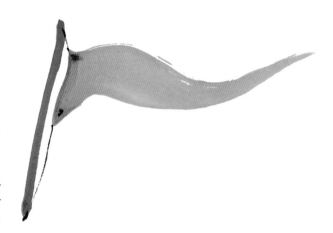

Line 4: There is real danger at work. Politicking and serious back-stabbing will cause you harm and distress. As a result your health and confidence take a severe beating. The best way to counter this period is to place a talisman or amulet at the office. Get the image of a rooster to quieten down all the noise (such images are said to be excellent at 'pecking away at troublemakers') and hang a painting of a mountain behind you. If you do not act fast you might find yourself manoeuvred out of a job.

Line 5: There is such good news for you if you obtain this changing line. It predicts that you will be getting excellent help from a powerful and influential person of the opposite sex. This leads to some brilliant achievements and forges a partnership deal for you that will bring happiness and success. Those seeking to get noticed at work will receive recognition and childless couples will soon conceive.

Line 6: This line offers only moderate success as difficulties continue to plague you. This is not a good time for those who are engrossed with their love life. Sweethearts could move away or find someone else. The advice from the I Ching is to be inactive and low key.

45 Ts'ui

Symbolizes gathering

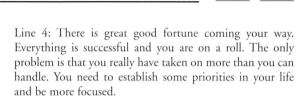

**Celebrations can create cause for strife
When gatherings of people
Are in numbers too large to control
The oracle advises to temper festivities with
    moderation**

A celebration, a party, a festival – all are indicated in this hexagram. There is enough cause for celebration and good fortune is easily predicted. Business prospects are favourable, while impending marriages meet with happy outcomes. But celebrations are best in moderation, for success breeds its own kind of strife.

Those who obtain this hexagram should not hesitate when it comes to seeking a meeting with someone important. The prospects for success are good and the meeting will be beneficial. Those presently engaged in a difficult undertaking should continue, for success is on the cards. It is not necessary to be discouraged. The time for celebrating is soon at hand. Those wishing to tie the knot are also advised to plan with great joyousness, for the hexagram symbolizes a happy gathering of people.

The Elements
Tui (metal) is above Kun (earth), a situation where earth produces metal. The relationship is productive and thus auspicious. The nuclear trigrams are Sun above Ken, a pairing of wood with earth, so the inner indications are destructive.

The Moving Lines
Line 1 (at the bottom): Caution is advised because initially there will be problems. Success comes much later, after a demanding period during which patience and hard work are called for.

Line 2: You will meet new people through important introductions and these will lead to profitable ventures. Your efforts will be fruitful, so there is every reason to celebrate.

Line 3: This line suggests only moderate success. There will be developments that cause problems and slow you down. As a result unhappiness and frustration follow.

Line 4: There is great good fortune coming your way. Everything is successful and you are on a roll. The only problem is that you really have taken on more than you can handle. You need to establish some priorities in your life and be more focused.

Line 5: There seems to be a credibility problem. You must try to convince others of your sincerity and good standing. Invest in mentor luck, for you are sorely lacking in this, and also activate your south sector. With some real effort you will succeed.

Line 6: Unfortunate developments at the macro level will affect your lifestyle. Bad luck will cause you distress and your health suffers. This is a good time to take a holiday and forget about work. When you return refreshed you will be better able to cope with the problems facing you.

46 Sheng

Symbolizes ascending

Chi ascending, reaching upwards
The plant grows, it matures and it flowers
It bears fruit
What can be more auspicious?

Here the Sheng or growth chi is precious and fruitful. It brings great good fortune and success. The image suggested is of a seed planted and nurtured to maturity, reflecting the natural order of the cosmos. But Sheng chi is more than just material success. Here the lines suggest a thrusting upward that is fuelled by your will and effort, a rise from humble circumstances to power and influence.

When you reach for the skies, your motivation ensures success. But it is the purity of intention that causes all obstacles to wither away. Thus growth by expansion is made possible not by arrogance but by humility and modesty. When attempting to scale the heights, it is beneficial to guard against over-confidence. Planning is also vital, as are helpful people, making a steady ascent possible.

The Elements
Earth is above wood, with the two elements in conflict, while the nuclear trigrams are Chen (wood) above Tui (metal). The long-term and hidden indications are dangerous, as metal destroys wood.

The Moving Lines
Line 1 (at the bottom): There is fantastic luck indicated and everything is blessed. This means that all your efforts will be fruitful, working out as planned and bringing you tremendous satisfaction. You can formulate plans to expand with confidence. Marriage will also meet with success.

Line 2: Bad luck can be transformed into good and things move smoothly. In love this has the potential to be a wonderful period, with two people pledging their love to each other. But if yours is an unequal relationship the indications are less auspicious.

Line 3: Careers will take off when you obtain this changing line. A new job offer is soon forthcoming and it will bring more money and greater prestige. You will not regret accepting it.

Line 4: This is a good time for those engaged in professional pursuits. You can expect a meaningful promotion soon, as you have caught the attention of a very powerful person. But be careful about being excessively eager and remember that the business world is a two-way street. The oracle also advises you not to sell yourself short.

Line 5: Steady steps up the career ladder are sometimes more fun than taking giant leaps. This is true regardless of your profession. But this line does spell success, with your efforts bearing fruit.

Line 6: Some setbacks and obstacles are coming to plague you, but they will be more like inconveniences and should not cause you distress. So put up with small problems and keep the bigger picture in sight.

47 K'un

Symbolizes oppression

Alas, the lake has run dry
And mankind is exhausted coping with obstacles
The superior man maintains his composure
And transforms adversity into good fortune

This hexagram indicates huge difficulties that impede growth as a result of new developments. Everywhere there are obstructions. Danger, quarrels and shortage of money have befallen you. On the left there is oppression and on the right corruption – the oracle is advising you to proceed with extreme caution.

It might be beneficial to move to another job, find another assignment, even perhaps change the friends you hang out with or move to another city. There does not seem much for you in your old haunts. In business it is perhaps necessary to rethink and formulate a new strategy. In your personal life this hexagram is saying 'take the plunge'. Your present situation does not seem to benefit you, so it might be a good idea to change course.

The Elements
Tui (metal) is above Kan (water), an exhaustive relationship, while the nuclear trigrams are Sun (wood) above Li (fire). Once again the relationship is exhaustive, so the inner meaning of this hexagram continues to indicate exhaustion, hence the advise to change course.

The Moving Lines
Line 1 (at the bottom): This looks like a dark period in your life – the indications are that the bad luck can last as long as three years. It is an excellent idea to revitalize the chi inside your home, office and bedroom. Use incense (lavender or sandalwood would be excellent) to clear away yin-drenched chi. Also use sounds: a crystal or a seven-metals singing bowl will improve your luck considerably. Having done that, stay low key and do not undertake journeys, sign contracts or expand.

Line 2: The advice is to postpone making all important decisions and to suspend all new expansions. Doing nothing is beneficial.

Line 3: Once again the line is inauspicious. Misfortunes, sadness and loss are all indicated. It is a good idea to investigate the chi of the house and to see if anything can be improved. The I Ching reflects the quality of energy in your home and when such inauspicious lines are received they often point to things being out of sync. Realigning the chi with Feng Shui changes will make a difference.

Line 4: There is grave danger indicated and you are advised to tread carefully. Do not commit to anything or anyone, as whatever is entered into during this time of bad chi will not be beneficial or have a good ending.

Line 5: You will need to make personal sacrifices in the near future. It will also be necessary to work extremely hard with discouragingly small rewards. But this is not a time to think big or be ambitious. The oracle is saying that you should be grateful for even small morsels of luck.

Line 6: There is no way out. Hampered by obstacles on all sides, alas, it seems that you might be better simply taking the drastic decision to change everything. This is because nothings benefits. At times like this you must analyse if something may be wrong with the quality of chi that surrounds you – especially whether there are poison arrows attacking your main door or where you sit at work.

48 Ching

Symbolizes the well

Look deep into the depths of the well
What you see is nourishment and water

This hexagram compares the image of the well to mankind. When a well is clean and properly maintained it gives forth pure and tasty water that nourishes. If it is neglected and old, the water will be dirty and murky, bringing illness and poisoning.

Dilapidated wells can be repaired and made productive again. It is the same with life. When you organize your affairs properly people cooperate and benefits accrue to everyone. Improvements bring progress and prosperity. This reasoning applies to all dimensions of life – in businesses as much as in relationships. There must be proper nurturing and care. Effort must be made to ensure that life moves on smoothly. If you do not understand this, you could attract the kind of misfortune that will cause havoc in your life.

Note also that old wells are a source of danger. When the rope breaks, for instance, you will not be able to get water. So the superior man always works diligently to improve his life.

The Elements

Kan (water) is above Sun (wood), and here wood exhausts water. The nuclear trigrams are Li (fire) above Tui (metal), a conflicting relationship. This means that both sets of trigrams are inauspicious.

The Moving Lines

Line 1 (at the bottom): This line describes an old well in need of repair. This suggests that whatever concerns you at the moment and is the subject of this consultation needs improvement. Even relationships need to be repaired when familiarity causes insensitivity to creep in, and careers need revitalizing when the daily grind of work makes you stale.

Line 2: The well is dry and the jug leaks, suggesting a very bad time indeed. Situations with loved ones and at the office are tense, with no respite in sight. It is necessary for you to take drastic action to improve the situation.

Line 3: It appears that your circumstances in life are improving. Your ideas for dealing with the situation in your life right now are sound, which means you can proceed with whatever you plan on doing. But be prepared for an uphill struggle.

Line 4: This line suggests a period of learning and gaining valuable experience. It is by improving yourself that you will be able to participate actively and favourably when opportunities occur. The idea is to be prepared for good things that are coming.

Line 5: There is success. All your hard work and efforts are rewarded. Profits flow in and you gain the respect of others. The image is of a well which provides clear, cold spring water, water that is even safe enough to drink.

Line 6: This line indicates great good fortune. Your work brings success. There is more money and you have every reason to feel good about yourself. The image here is of a dependable well whose spring water will never run dry. Those getting this line can take heart from the oracle's words of encouragement: 'Here is a really great man whose inner wealth truly is inexhaustible.' And the more others draw from him/her the greater that wealth becomes.

49 Ko

Symbolizes revolution

In the lake there is a fire
Upheaval occurs because water and fire conflict
An impossible situation must be changed

Situations of conflict get out of hand and lead to major upheavals. There is fire in the lake, so this hexagram is describing a group of people who have such serious differences of opinion they come to blows. Disagreements and violent friction create strife and conflict – an altogether unstable situation. There is dire need for change and for leadership, but there is also danger. This hexagram is a sign of danger and getting it is a warning.

The Elements
Tui (metal) is above Li (fire), a destructive relationship that suggests conflict and combat. The nuclear trigrams are Chien (metal) above Sun (wood), a destructive relationship which suggests danger lurks.

The Moving Lines
Line 1 (at the bottom): Guard against over-ambition for this leads to a great deal of opposition from those around you. Do not think you can depend on your abilities alone, for luck is not necessarily with you. Adopt a very humble posture and refrain from appearing arrogant.

Line 2: You are ready to take your rightful place as a leader. It is time now to act, as good fortune is on your side.

Demonstrate both your courage and your conviction, but also pace yourself. Make your moves one at a time.

Line 3: There is confusion and politics turn nasty. For someone who is inexperienced, it is hard to stay calm and unaffected by the lies and counter-lies that the situation is revealing. But you must stay calm, for squabbling and petty rivalries need to be dealt with. It is the man who remains unruffled by betrayal who will win the day.

Line 4: A leader emerges. It can be you, in which case be prepared for the great challenges that lie ahead. If not you, then someone close to you becomes the leader. Give him your fullest support, for the future is looking bright. Remorse vanishes with the morning sunshine. There can be no regrets, only a looking ahead to reap the rich harvest.

Line 5: A great man is like a tiger. He is highly respected despite his occasional display of teeth. Righteous anger and wrathful responses are suited to the times and the circumstances. Such a leader demonstrates potential for brilliance, but it is necessary to be dynamic and also nimble for there are traps all along the way.

Line 6: This line strongly urges you to stay on course. To persist in your efforts is what will bring good fortune. Writers will gain recognition and righteous behaviour will bring its own rewards.

50 Ting

Symbolizes the cauldron

Where there is a lake nearby
Wood fuels the fire, producing steam
The superior man writes his own destiny
Combining heaven and earth luck
Bringing the two into harmony

This hexagram looks like a cauldron, with fire above fuelled by the wood below. The nuclear trigram is water creating steam, which is energy and nourishment. Supreme good fortune springs from the cauldron, which is also the symbol of offerings to the gods.

Success must surely materialize, given such auspicious circumstances. The superior man creates his own destiny, combining his observations with his innate goodness to benefit everyone. Thus from auspicious circumstances come equally auspicious results.

The Elements
Fire is above wood, an exhaustive relationship, while the nuclear trigrams are Tui above Chien (metal or gold doubled), so the indications are extremely auspicious.

The Moving Lines
Line 1 (at the bottom): This line indicates a second wife or a love affair, so there is sadness but also happiness for others. Initial disappointment leads to later triumphs.

Line 2: There is plenty of food and prosperity abounds. Envious people cast the evil eye, so you must be careful.

Place a suitable coin pa kua amulet inside your purse or wear it to dispel the influence of jealous colleagues so you are not affected by their envy.

Line 3: This is a very trying time when things will go wrong, inconveniencing you and slowing you down. But don't worry, as upset will become success and opportunities will open up new avenues to you. Just stay relaxed and do not overreact.

Line 4: This is a line of loss and misfortune. Injury happens to you and illness overtakes you. Get the chi around you properly analysed to ensure you are not suffering from bad Feng Shui time stars.

Line 5: This line offers brilliant indications of success, when everything works out fine and life moves along smoothly. There are more friends than enemies and your social life sees a marked upward swing. If you see butterflies it suggests that a transformation is taking place. If the butterfly enters your home it is even more auspicious. It means helpful people will assist you.

Line 6: Great good fortune is coming to you. The imagery is of raining jade and gold pieces by the thousand. Surely with such a line you have the courage to proceed strongly forward and to generate a genuinely confident attitude. Sometimes it is the expectation of success that creates the energy for success to materialize.

51 Chen

Symbolizes thunder

The clap of thunder arouses
An entire countryside, yet it lasts
Only for a brief moment and then is gone
Like fame, success, acclaim
All of life is impermanent

This hexagram evokes the image of thunder, creating shock and fear. Thunder goes deep into people's souls and often shakes them into action.

Wonderful luck is predicted for those in the entertainment, sports and publicity-related fields – anything requiring the luck of fame and recognition. There is merry-making and a sense of joyousness attached to this hexagram. If you are filled with energy and enthusiasm you will feel an affinity with its whole ambience.

However, it is also good to temper enthusiasm with restraint. Thunder is loud and it brings success, chasing away all bad luck from your life, but when it is doubled, it brings shock and fear. Then success turns to a need for caution. Excess of any kind and in any form is seldom positive all the time.

The Elements
Wood doubled are the elements here, with both upper and lower primary trigrams Chen. The nuclear trigrams are Kan (water) above Ken (earth), a destructive relationship.

The Moving Lines
Line 1 (at the bottom): This line describes a situation where one may feel a sudden crisis of confidence or attack of insecurity. There is no need for this, as the line indicates good fortune. There will be good news.

Line 2: The danger indicated by this line is real. Loss of wealth, sickness and misfortunes are ahead, and although the bad times last only a short while and there is an eventual return to normality, it is advisable to take precautions and wear protective amulets.

Line 3: This line advises you to be circumspect in your response to new friends and acquaintances. It is only by being wary and alert that you will avoid getting hurt. People are not what they appear and first impressions can be deceptive.

Line 4: You are obviously stuck in a rut, so it is better to not do anything for a while. Boredom is infinitely better than danger.

Line 5: This line offers neither good nor bad news, so it is better to do what you are doing presently and to take no risks. This is not a time to stick your neck out or to invest effort in new ventures. There is little to recommend such a course of action.

Line 6: This is a dangerous time and you definitely need to be extra careful. You must strenuously avoid getting entangled in new situations. Do not volunteer to do any good deeds as these will surely backfire and learn to stay out of other people's affairs.

52 Ken

Symbolizes stillness

When the time comes for keeping still
The superior man's thoughts turn inwards
Reflecting the self
He searches for the eternal source

This hexagram is mountain or earth doubled. The image is of immobility and stillness, so it suggests a time of introspection and meditation. It also indicates planning and building self-reliance. When you take stock of your life, it suggests a time of consolidation, clearing out the clutter that muddies your view. It is not a time to expand, so if you obtain this hexagram take its advice and keep still. In love this means do not make any fresh commitments. In business it indicates not committing to new product lines, new people or new strategies. It seems better to stay old-fashioned and a little bit behind others.

Those who get this hexagram to a serious question might want to consider taking a short break to a place of mountains. The sight of the Swiss Alps or the Himalayan mountains of Kathmandu will inspire you. The oracle is excellent for pointing the way. The next best thing to going to the mountains is to hang up a painting of one with which you feel an affinity.

The Elements
Both upper and lower trigrams are Ken (earth doubled), which means mountain and belongs to the element of earth. The nuclear trigrams are Chen (wood) above Kan (water), a productive relationship, which indicates that in the end good fortune will prevail.

The Moving Lines
Line 1 (at the bottom): There are no immediate threats to your existence but now it is not a good time to pursue new ventures.

Line 2: Tiredness and lethargy indicate that you are exhausting yourself too much. When you feel sleepy all the time it is hard to concentrate and life itself appears boring and uninspiring. You will have to shake yourself out of this horrible phase.

Line 3: A case of simply trying too hard. Sometimes when you are slow but steady you will complete your assignment with flying colours. If you attempt too much speed it will often be at the expense of caution.

Line 4: The advice is not to be aggressive. Progress and advancement do not appear feasible. Dreams of getting promotion will also have to be put on hold for the immediate future.

Line 5: This line indicates a breakthrough and success in your undertakings. This is a time when whatever you do will bring benefits and advancement. Be on the lookout for opportunities. If you donate to charity, do so today and your good fortune will be enhanced.

Line 6: This line suggests good fortune. There are gains in investments and luck on the stockmarkets, so gains are easy to come by. At work there is recognition of your contribution, so this is a period of satisfaction. Life seems very agreeable indeed.

53 Chien

Symbolizes gradual development

Trees appear tall and stately
By the side of the mountain
Growing gradually and gracefully
They are seen for miles around

This hexagram describes how respect and influence usually come to those who are patient and honourable. Like trees growing slowly on the mountainside, when your rise has been gradual and solid, your success will be built on strong foundations and thus attract great respect.

Despite obstacles and difficulties, goals are usually achieved. This applies equally to career development, the gradual progress of a love relationship, business and studies. When everything happens too fast, foundations are weak and the danger is that success could be superficial. If you obtain this hexagram and you want to extract some growth energy from a tall and healthy tree, here is what you can do. Take a walk in the park and look for a strong tree, one you feel a close affinity with. Go and sit under it for a while, closing your eyes and tuning your mind to synchronize with that of the tree. Then stand up and, using both arms, embrace the tree and feel it pass on its wonderful benevolent chi to you. Visualize the energy as an invisible and divine yellow light. Close your eyes lightly if you find this helps. You need to hold the tree for only 30 seconds or so. If you feel a real affinity growing between you and the tree, visit it often. Taoists believe that when the time is right all of us can find our spiritual guides in the trees, the stones and the earth.

The Elements
Sun above signifies wood while the trigram below is Ken signifying earth. Here wood destroys earth signifying a situation of destruction. Wood uses up the goodness of the earth resulting in a depletion. The nuclear trigrams symbolize Li (fire) above Kan (water) – a situation of direct conflict.

The Moving Lines
Line 1 (at the bottom): This is a line of difficulty, indicating danger and misfortune to a boy or young man. But with perseverance ultimately there will be good fortune.

Line 2: There is good luck in your development and also plenty to eat. You can be comfortable in everything.

Line 3: Misfortune is suggested in this line and ventures cannot succeed, like a flower bud full of promise suddenly dying on an unexpectedly hot day. Failure can come suddenly and without warning. Those who are expecting a child must take good care, otherwise there might be some misfortune associated with descendants luck.

Line 4: There is great harmony and goodwill at home but outside you could meet with difficulties in dealing with colleagues and business associates. There is minor good fortune and it is necessary to enhance the home with symbols of good fortune.

Line 5: Your success comes in the wake of three years' preparation and waiting. There is good fortune and the completion of a project which could well catapult you into a different league. Do not get too carried away by your breakthrough success. Instead, be ready to take on the next step. Prepare yourself.

Line 6: There is significant success, as well as unexpected opportunities in your career. Those who have just enjoyed a rise in status may not be ready to take on additional responsibilities and duties. Expectations of you will have increased. Do not allow this new pressure to floor you. Life is filled with opportunities and the superior man is one who adjusts his attitude according to the good fortune that comes.

54 Kuei Mei

Symbolizes marrying girl

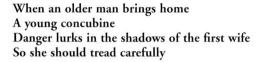

When an older man brings home
A young concubine
Danger lurks in the shadows of the first wife
So she should tread carefully

This hexagram warns of supreme danger at work and in your personal life. The imagery used is of a young concubine being brought into a traditional household where her fate is uncertain, despite being loved by the man of the house. Her well-being is so easily undermined, for her rank is well beneath that of the principal wife.

This is true also in the modern workplace. When you have been hired by the big boss, do not mistakenly believe you rank equally to his aides, who are already part of his inner cabinet. Unless you succeed in forging alliances with the older staff, your life could be made quite miserable. Your work can easily be sabotaged and you can be defeated within an environment you know nothing about.

The Elements
Chen (wood) is above and Tui (metal) is below, a situation that appears destructive. The nuclear trigrams indicate Kan (water) above Li (fire), an inherently destructive relationship which can be transformed by superior men into a situation of great power. Generally this relationship suggests ultimate disaster.

The Moving Lines
Line 1 (at the bottom): This line suggests different good things for different scenarios, depending on the question being asked. For those at work and about to set forth on their career, it predicts a mentor who will take you under their wing. For those asking about their love life, there is a new romantic interest coming your way. And for those taking examinations, the results are good.

Line 2: This is a very unspectacular period indeed. Neither misfortune nor bad luck plague you, yet you have little to celebrate.

Line 3: There are sudden advances and also sudden setbacks, causing you to feel unbalanced and unsure of yourself. This is all part of the situation you find yourself embroiled in. You must be careful of hidden enemies and unworthy fair-weather friends. The latter can often be far more deadly than the former.

Line 4: This line suggests a period of waiting will be very beneficial. This is because a better opportunity or deal will come at a later date and there is nothing to be lost by waiting. If you are planning a business trip, this is a good time as there will be many good things coming your way. But gains are not instant. Opportunities must still be developed before they bear fruit.

Line 5: There are favourable indications for high-profile successes ahead, the kind that bring a certain glamour and publicity as well. But the good fortune is real despite the veneer of glitz. By all means applaud! Also, don't forget to enjoy what you have worked so hard to achieve.

Line 6: This line indicates empty promises made to you by dishonourable people. Do not be taken in by sweet-talking older men. They are not to be trusted and following them will put you and perhaps your loved ones in grave danger. You cannot expect success in any new job, new relationship or new venture. Better to pass and wait for something better to come along.

55 Feng

Symbolizes greatness

Lightning flashes across the night sky
Blinding one and all with its brilliance
Even the king is impressed

This hexagram describes an attainment of great brilliance. Here the image is of lightning streaking magnificently across the night skies, accompanied by thunder and great brightness. So brilliant success is indicated – the kind that will make even the king sit up and take notice.

Here is a couple in their prime: a man who dazzles with his genius, a woman who impresses with her luminosity and radiance. There is also plenty of cash.

But beware, for by its very nature lightning is impermanent – a moment of glory and then no more. The time of abundance is all too often brief, so it is necessary to guard against being over-confident. You should not be dazzled by your own success. Success comes fast but it can also desert you as quickly. The superior man maintains his humility and internal character in the face of applause. For the sage who expects success to be transitory, it is then continuous. Greatness achieved becomes long-lasting and the respect of mankind continues throughout life. If you notice that the day is especially bright and the sun is shining brilliantly, or there is thunder and lightning, both weather indications confirm the predictions of this hexagram, which is that abundance and great success are coming.

The Elements

Wood is above fire, an exhaustive relationship, which suggests it is better to rest than to be active. The nuclear trigrams are Tui (metal) above Sun (wood), also a potentially destructive pairing. The indications are negative. Make the most of your success, for it will be gone all too soon, to be replaced by exhaustion and perhaps even a downfall.

The Moving Lines

Line 1 (at the bottom): Good fortune is indicated and people help you. There are influential friends in your life right now, but beware, for even in the midst of success and glamour the enemy lurks. You need to be ever watchful and alert. In love you could have a secret competitor for the affections of your sweetheart.

Line 2: You will attain success under adverse conditions. On the surface things appear disheartening, but your luck is excellent, so everything works out well.

Line 3: There are hidden enemies working against you. Something is standing in the way of your success. Be alert to mischief-makers who want to cause you problems.

Line 4: Hard work leads to the successful attainment of goals. It is unnecessary to grow too fast or move too quickly to advance your relationship with people, be they lovers or colleagues. Better to go slowly, otherwise you will only stumble and fall. Misunderstandings and instability will then be the result.

Line 5: Honour, power and influence are all indicated by this line and it is a time of supreme good fortune. Anyone obtaining line 5 of this hexagram must prepare themselves for additional responsibilities, as they will be approached by influential people to take on a leadership role. Be prepared for greater glory. Stay humble!

Line 6: This indicates a period of decline for someone who has already achieved success or is prosperous. It is a good idea to do something charitable to stem the tide. By donating to a worthwhile charity, it is possible to delay or at least reduce the bad luck. For those who are in a stage of growth and preparation, however, this is an excellent line. Those taking examinations, for example, will do extremely well.

56 Lu

Symbolizes the exile

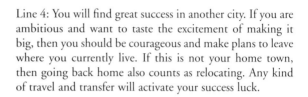

The lonely traveller
Stays upright and is clear-minded
Then he maintains his inner dignity

This hexagram indicates good news for those who travel for their living – sales reps and traders – but it is unfavourable for marriage, embarking on new ventures or entering into business or other kinds of partnership.

All parties to any kind of partnership will eventually change their minds. There is no permanence possible and the relationship will be racked with misunderstandings and hostility. Alas, in essence the wanderer – the image of this hexagram – is a loner, someone who needs and desires space. Thus loneliness and separation are ahead of anyone obtaining this hexagram.

The Elements
Li (fire) is above Ken (earth), a productive relationship that augurs well for the present. The nuclear trigrams are Kan (water) above Sun (wood), an exhaustive relationship.

The Moving Lines
Line 1 (at the bottom): A lack of energy and willpower is suggested by this line, like a wanderer who does not quite know where the final destination will be. There is a heavy sense of being alone. Perhaps you might meet someone who will show you the way, but your successes are small. There is a higher probability of misfortune. So be careful before embarking on a journey or a new project.

Line 2: You will obtain recognition away from your homeland if you get this line. Any kind of travel or change of location will benefit you. A transfer to another part of the country or even abroad will bring good fortune. You can use your love of adventure and the unknown to benefit your career as well as your personal life. If you are unmarried, relocating will bring an unexpected bonus.

Line 3: This line suggests that fire above the mountain will bring disaster. Here the trigram above is Li (fire) while the trigram is Ken (earth), which also stands for the mountain. This is a time when there is danger for you personally, as well as to what you stand for, so you must expect to face some serious trouble.

Line 4: You will find great success in another city. If you are ambitious and want to taste the excitement of making it big, then you should be courageous and make plans to leave where you currently live. If this is not your home town, then going back home also counts as relocating. Any kind of travel and transfer will activate your success luck.

Line 5: A wonderful line, this indicates that you will enjoy a brilliant success which brings prestige, power and extra money. You cannot ask for more, as it is like having your dreams come true. You should not allow this brilliant success to go to your head, however, and do not forget those who have helped you get this far.

Line 6: Misfortune is suggested by this line – a risk of financial loss. On the surface you could be fooled into thinking that everything is going smoothly, but a deep betrayal of your trust is taking place. Open your eyes and do not be too gullible.

57 Sun

Symbolizes the wind

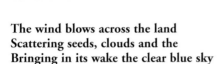

**The wind blows across the land
Scattering seeds, clouds and the
Bringing in its wake the clear blue sky**

This is one of the eight hexagrams of the I Ching that is made up of the same trigram doubled. In this case it is Sun, indicating wood energy at its zenith, caused by the preponderance of the powerful blasts of wind chi.

This hexagram signifies dust being blown by the wind. It settles on a faraway mountain. The image is of the width and breadth of the land, of the distances covered by the wind and of the height of the mountains. The hexagram indicates that success must be found elsewhere, in another part of the country or even abroad. There is a suggestion of contemplation, of taking the macro view like a bird flying above the land and seeing a vision that is all-encompassing.

When the power of the wind is equated with that of a person, it suggests someone of great charisma. Such a person is surely a ruler, a king, a leader of mankind. This hexagram is excellent for anyone contemplating a career in politics, for it predicts an evolution of personality so impressive that there will be huge success. People will be swayed by his/her words in the same way that the grass is swayed by the force of the wind. There will be sacrifice still to come and a sincerity of motive is called for. The wind blowing signifies the need to observe and learn.

Nothing penetrates like the wind, and nothing is as effective in dispersing the clouds or the dust that covers the gold of the ground. The wind brings bright clear skies. It is suggestive of news travelling far and wide. There are fame and recognition, in the same way as an uncovering of motives and intentions.

The hexagram indicates success when you have a good product, a good strategy or even a good leader to follow. But not otherwise. The wind is a double-edged sword that brings recognition of both good and bad. So whether one succeeds or not depends on more than just good luck.

Only the genuine article will meet genuine success. Prosperity is achieved when there is real skill, talent and strategy behind your words. This hexagram does, however, favour both investments that are made overseas, and relocating to a new place to live. It favours those seeking new markets for their products. There is also good fortune for those planning to marry someone from another country.

The Elements

The primary trigrams are both Sun, so the effect is wood doubled. The nuclear trigrams are Li (fire) above Tui (metal). The essence of this hexagram is what you make of it.

The Moving Lines

Line 1 (at the bottom): Mixed signals are confusing you but this is because your situation attracts both ups and downs. There will thus be some gains and some losses, but in the end you will have the success you plan for.

Line 2: Honesty and sincerity are the values that bring you success, like the wind that scatters good seeds which take root and produce healthy plants. You know that the future looks bright for you, but there is no need to keep asking. Your worst enemy is your feeling of insecurity. Rein in your uncertainties and move bravely forward. As long as you are honourable, you will become a superior person.

Line 3: Travel is indicated by this line and seeing the 'great man' holds the key to success. But there are also hidden enemies working against you. There could be sudden loss or unexpected humiliation. It is important to be extra careful. Wear a personal talisman or amulet to protect you.

Line 4: Remorse vanishes as instability dries up. You are now entering a time when benefits and good news come continuously. There is cause for rejoicing and celebrations.

Line 5: This is a great line as everything indicated is positive. Your abilities find expression in stunning fashion. There will be extra responsibilities and promotion. Do not be afraid of accepting what appears risky and difficult. It is only by rising to the challenge that you will be able to demonstrate your superiority.

Line 6: This line indicates a loss of wealth. If you persist in following your way, there will be loss and sufferings. You could also fall ill and succumb to weakness of the joints. Be less dogmatic in your attitudes. In humility lie the seeds of conciliation and eventual success.

58 Tui

Symbolizes joyousness

Tui is joyousness and good news
The image of the beautiful lake and the young lady
Savour special moments like this
For, alas, they do not come often

Rejoicing creates magical momentum. It is infectious, creating its own excitement. But do not let joyousness degenerate into uncontrolled mirth, for then what is gentle and graceful can easily become unsavoury and decadent. The hexagram comprises the trigram Tui doubled, and the intrinsic quality of Tui is the gentility of the youngest maiden in the household. This hexagram implies there will be great happiness in the family. Beauty, success and many good things are coming. This includes gold or wealth, so it is the kind of good fortune that brings smiles to faces.

The Elements

The primary trigrams are both Tui, so the effect is a doubling of metal, which can also stand for gold. The nuclear trigrams are Sun (wood) above Li (fire), so the relationship is productive and thus excellent to the core.

The Moving Lines

Line 1 (at the bottom): There are both harmony and affinity between you and those close to you. With no problem worth mentioning your life is truly blessed.

Line 2: This line suggests that your path is bright and clear. You are one of the fortunate ones who need never plan too far ahead. You were born with the pearl luck in your mouth.

Line 3: A series of little problems will irritate and nag you but bear with it, because in a month or so they will all evaporate. There really is something wonderful waiting for you, so for the moment stay humble and bide your time. Remember that everything happens in a cycle and when you are experiencing good times there will have to be some payback.

Line 4: This line advises you to be less showy about your material success. There are envious eyes watching and they will have the opportunity to get at you. As a result there is no harmony or peace in your life at this time. You will need to learn patience and to understand that having your material assets thrown in their face will not endear you to those less fortunate than you. Sure, your success continues, but to enjoy your life the key is humility and being less of a show-off.

Line 5: This line warns you that an unknown enemy is working against you, undermining your best efforts. You do not know who it is, but even if you did there is nothing much you can do to stem the flow of half-truths and slander that is making your life miserable. Place a rooster image on your desk (such images are said to be excellent at 'pecking away at troublemakers') and wear a personal amulet. This should at least substantially reduce the negative effects.

Line 6: Someone is plotting against you but you are blissfully unaware of it. However, there is little to worry about, for someone very influential is on your side. This person will place you in a completely different league. The oracle advises you to focus on your work and your relationships. Whatever you do, do not respond to negative arrows that are sent your way.

59 Huan

Symbolizes dispersion

Wind blows over water
Creating mist that transforms
Even dust into jewels

This hexagram describes an image of gentle wind blowing over water, suggesting there are benefits in 'crossing the waters'. Here perseverance and a focused goal are called for. With these twin attributes in place, success and advancement are sure to follow. But separation is also indicated, as are travel and a dispersal of energy. The oracle advises aggressive expansion beyond the shores of your own country. Travel, relocation, going abroad – for business, for your career or to further your education – all are favourable.

But while work-related indications are positive, there will be misfortune in your love life and in your love relationships. Any relocation could lead to an end of your marriage or, if you are not married but dating, put a strain on your relationship. If you are unattached this hexagram has nothing much to offer in terms of encouragement.

The Elements
Sun above signifies wood while the trigram below is Kan signifying water. Here water creates wood signifying a situation of production, which indicates enhancement. Water enhances the wood element bringing excellent growth energy. Wood growing always signifies expansion. The nuclear trigrams symbolize Ken (earth) above Chen (wood) – a situation of unexpected misfortune.

The Moving Lines
Line 1 (at the bottom): The image here is of boats sailing smoothly across water. You will shortly receive the letter you are waiting for, telling you the outcome of your application for either a job or a place at a foreign college, and the answer is positive. Success in your projects is indicated.

Line 2: Be alert to opportunities and look beyond your traditional boundaries, because there are many good things waiting for you but they may not be where you think they are. For instance, if you are looking for a job do not confine your search to one industry. Expand your horizons, but be discerning. You can afford to be choosy, as success awaits you.

Line 3: Guard against being over-confident and over-indulgent. There are frivolous friends in your midst and harmless envy can turn into harmful jealousy very easily. Take care not to be too trusting.

Line 4: When you have a sound strategy you will attain the goals you have laid out for yourself. Both circumstances and timing are working in your favour. Trust your instincts.

Line 5: There is good fortune awaiting you. Your undertakings will bring you honour and prestige. It is worth working hard because you are will reap the rewards.

Line 6: This is a good time to be positive and to move strongly ahead. Stay cool and make sure you do not lose control over your future. At times of success it is easy to get carried away, so stay grounded and do not lose sight of your ambitions.

60 Chieh

Symbolizes limitation

When waters rise to overflowing
A source of good becomes dangerous
Life is the same
When its parameters are breached, there is danger

This is a hexagram that stresses the need always to live within your means and act within your limits. When you break the banks of your livelihood, you will lose control and then disaster can easily follow. It is important to think before speaking, to plan before acting. This way you will not overspend or commit beyond your limits.

This hexagram also advocates the need for compromise. The oracle suggests that there is little merit in testing your limits or being so extreme in your attitudes that you end up alienating those close to you. Often, taking the middle ground is the best way. So set your limits, be clear about your limitations, stay within them and then move ahead with confidence. Also remember that your ambitions should also stay within the limits of your capabilities.

The Elements
Kan (water) is above Tui (metal), a productive and therefore auspicious relationship. The nuclear trigrams are Ken (earth) above Chen (wood) and here the relationship is destructive, indicating danger beyond.

The Moving Lines
Line 1 (at the bottom): This is not a time to take risks unnecessarily. You should be satisfied with your current situation. It is by knowing the limits that define your lifestyle at the present moment that you will have some small success.

Line 2: You should stay alert to new opportunities that keep coming your way. Do not miss them as you have to take action before they can transform into something wonderful. Success is certain as you have the good fortune to succeed, but you must plant the seed before it can flower and fruit.

Line 3: Be careful of over-indulging yourself. It is so easy to get carried away by your own excesses. You must also know that there are troublemakers within your circle of friends, so be careful.

Line 4: There is virtue in being contented with life. Often this can lead to success that falls into your lap. Relax and accept the good fortune that comes your way. If you get this line, going with the flow is the best approach. If you are too tense all the good luck meant for you will simply slip through your fingers.

Line 5: The humble person who focuses on others is certain to succeed. This is a line of great good fortune, for your work will bring you honour, position and power. You also benefit from the loyalty of colleagues and co-workers. There is much goodwill being sent your way.

Line 6: This line indicates that you are feeling weary. You want to give up, tired of the daily problems you have to cope with, but persevere, for there is much to benefit when you keep going. Soon whatever regrets or remorse you feel will vanish. There is much to be gained by being positive.

61 Chung Fu

Symbolizes inner truth

**A heart free of prejudice
Is always open to the inner truth**

This hexagram addresses the preciousness of having a sincere and true friend, someone you can trust and depend on. This is also the most precious of qualities to look for when we examine the relationships in our lives. Usually it is not so much opinions on issues that bond people as the genuineness of their friendship. Without sincerity, nothing exists to hold the friendship together.

If you obtain this hexagram the meaning is excellent, for it suggests sincerity and harmony. All members of a family get along and there is goodwill that can withstand even the harshest of challenges. This hexagram also applies to office relationships, between bosses and subordinates and between co-workers and colleagues. Success comes with cooperation.

This hexagram also points out that very often it is 'with the heart's overflow that the mouth speaks'. When the heart is free of prejudices and negative attitudes the truth comes forth easily, but when your inner mind harbours bad thoughts these always reveal themselves. If you get this hexagram and you have good motives, you are certain to succeed in what you do. But when you have hidden agendas, beware the consequences when these are revealed through your own indiscretions.

The Elements
The primary trigrams Sun (wood) above Tui (metal) suggest a destructive relationship, for metal destroys wood. The nuclear trigrams are Ken (earth) above Chen (wood), so the relationships of both sets of trigrams are inauspicious. This suggests that the state of inner truth does not last.

The Moving Lines
Line 1 (at the bottom): It would be advisable to work hard and stay low key, for hidden within your good fortune lurks danger. Beware of the tall poppy syndrome: try not to stand out too much, for it merely attracts envy and anger from lesser mortals. Life is seldom static and you will find as circumstances change so too do people's attitudes. Do not let friends of long-standing who turn against you stop you trusting others.

Line 2: It is likely that if you are pregnant you will have sons. This is a very good omen indeed and if you had an auspicious dream of children or a celebration then the oracle confirms that you will shortly have reason to celebrate. If you get this line and you encountered a little boy or saw a picture of a baby boy it also means that someone dear to you or even you yourself is about to conceive a baby.

Line 3: This line reflects the inner essence of the I Ching. If your fortunes have been good for the past few months, this line predicts a change and you might well suffer some setback. Likewise, if you have been having bad luck for the past few months, this line predicts a change and good fortune will follow a period of stagnation.

Line 4: This line is excellent for those who are concerned about their careers and their professional future. There are success and promotion. Students getting this line should also be happy about their examination results. However, in matters of the heart, this line does not suggest anything except loss. Indeed, married couples who are having troubles could end up losing each other.

Line 5: Once again this line brings good news. There is great good fortune promised to those engaged in business or about to start a new project. There will be many outstanding opportunities to increase your income and enhance your status. Goals are easily achieved and even enemies become friends. So this is a good time to consider diversifying into other careers and livelihoods, and even to enter the political arena. Since your luck is good, this is the time to 'go for it'.

Line 6: This line warns you against becoming entangled with someone who is a stranger. Do not be overly friendly to people you have just met as they could spell misfortune. Also beware of strangers bearing gifts – this line suggests there could be real danger.

62 Hsiao Kuo

Symbolizes small error or weakness

Small mistakes can hamper
The achievement of great things
Then it is time for exceptional prudence

This hexagram indicates a weakness – perhaps a skill inadequacy or a simple shortcoming – that can significantly hamper your success. If you are in a position of power or status, with both authority and responsibility, this hexagram suggests that you might not be up to the job. In this case it advises you to be extraordinarily humble and prudent. When you adopt such a demeanour, your inadequacies will be viewed as small errors and are easily forgiven and overlooked. But when you attempt to cover your inadequacies with rhetoric and arrogance, reaction from others is hostile and failure can result.

The hexagram recommends that you adopt such a posture of humility. Couch your silence with the dignity of diffidence, but also be aware that great success may not be easily achieved since there is a perceived weakness. The required strength or skill seems lacking, so it is a good idea not to set your sights too high.

If you see a bird soaring into the bright blue sky today, especially before you consult the oracle, it reinforces this message. The imagery of this hexagram is of a bird bringing a message. If the bird is seen flying into the sky, the message is that your ambitions are too high for you at this time. But if the bird flies to earth and, better yet, decends to a nest among trees or buildings, it is a good sign, suggesting that you are properly grounded in your attitude and will thus achieve slow but steady success.

The Elements

Chen (wood) is above Ken (earth), a relationship that suggests a certain negativity because the elements are in a destructive relationship. The nuclear trigrams are Tui (metal) above Sun (wood), also a destructive relationship.

The Moving Lines

Line 1 (at the bottom): You will enjoy rapid advancements at the beginning but the line reveals severe humiliation at a later date. What is suggested is that your conduct is excessively false – in mourning the laments are just too loud. Perhaps you should rethink your approach and make an effort to change your attitude.

Line 2: This line suggests you will be the beneficiary of favours from powerful and influential friends. Good luck is definitely on your side as there is an aura of goodwill surrounding you. Make full use of this good period in order to advance your career.

Line 3: This line indicates there is misfortune just around the corner. In what you plan to do, someone may stab you in the back, and you should be especially mindful of sweet-talking but false friends. As you tend to be rather naïve about how far people will go to advance themselves, at the expense of even their best friends, you could fall victim to this sort of betrayal. You should not be so trusting.

Line 4: The advice given here is to maintain the status quo. Whatever it is you are asking the oracle, the answer is to stay as you are. Later, when the time is more auspicious, you can proceed with fewer doubts. For now, enjoy the lifestyle you have achieved so far.

Line 5: This is definitely not the time to be taking risks, either with your money, your reputation or your heart! Accept the present conditions, otherwise there could be cause for regret. Let time help you ride out this bad period. To try to do something about it will only make matters worse.

Line 6: Be careful not to develop aspirations inside your head that are impossible to achieve. While it is good to dream, it is important that you do not delude yourself – nothing hurts more than being so ambitious that, instead of letting your determination strengthen you, you are weakened by having unrealistic aspirations.

63 Chi Chi

Symbolizes completion

**When water hangs over fire
Energy comes from the production of steam
Perfect equilibrium brings completion and then
Even fire and water create good fortune**

This hexagram indicates something successfully achieved – a project or business deal, a stage in your life, school or college studies.

Your life has reached one stage of equilibrium and you are making ready for the next. Life seems almost too perfect, so it is a good idea to watch out for creeping danger. This does not mean that you should live in fear, but you must not allow yourself to fall into a state of complete and utter decadence. Keep mind and body alert.

The I Ching always warns you to be careful when life has reached a stage when everything seems perfect. According to the oracle, the cosmic universe is never static, so circumstances and situations can always change. The superior man is aware of this truth and, in accepting it, is never caught unawares. In the flush of your happiness and success, therefore, leave some room for contemplation. Allow the philosopher in you to surface.

The Elements
Kan (water) is above Li (fire) and, because of the positioning of the elements, what seems to be a destructive relationship has been transformed into an auspicious one. The nuclear trigrams are Li above Kan, a reversal of places for the elements. Here the relationship is destructive, as water puts out the fire.

The Moving Lines
Line 1 (at the bottom): When one is cautious one is always prepared, but in this case all the preparation in the world cannot bring you big success. You will have to be content with small success at this stage of your development.

Line 2: Do not allow early setbacks to discourage you. Success is sure to come, but you need to be patient and persevere for it to happen.

Line 3: There are difficulties that will tax even the most determined and focused of people. The oracle advises you to relax and take things easy. After a short break from your work you will be ready to rise to the challenge. At this stage focusing on the family brings benefits.

Line 4: Be very cautious – when too much success comes too fast, you will be unable to cope with adversity and problems. Take a deep breath and attack your problems head on. You never know what you are capable of until you try and in so doing rise to the challenge.

Line 5: There is good news about small projects but grand schemes just cannot get off the ground. You must understand that being a visionary can be very lonely. Not everyone is able to see what you see. There is also the jealousy factor. If you are already successful, prosperous or influential, accept that you have enemies who will not want you to advance any further.

Line 6: You must try to postpone any travel that takes you overseas as there is danger. If you have to go, make sure you wear a protective travel amulet. There is also danger at work. Beware of a situation arising that is potentially damaging to you. Place a rooster image on your table (such images are said to be excellent at 'pecking away at troublemakers').

64 Wei Chi

Symbolizes before completion

The fox walks over the icy river
Any time the ice may break
He must tread slowly and be wary
And so must you

This hexagram describes a dangerous situation when conditions for survival are difficult. You may or may not rise to the occasion, but it is a tough time for you. What is called for is not so much hard work as a good strategy and a diplomatic attitude. Like the fox walking on ice, you need to tread carefully, always making certain you do not tread on anyone's toes. This is not a time to be foolishly brave. Boldness could lead to sudden death. Instead this is a time to go slowly, to forge helpful alliances and to find new benefactors. When you negotiate, appear to compromise with good grace.

This is the time before completion. Remember, the end is near and all that is needed is a final effort to take you to the next level. As long as you can keep your head above water, you will do just fine. Perseverance will bring good fortune. Be observant of your surroundings today. Tune in to your environment and take note of anything unusual. Whatever you see will reinforce aspects of the advice being given. When you open your conscious mind to your inner mind, it will communicate with you by making you more aware of your surroundings. So if you see something positive today be encouraged and guided by it. Let your instincts tell you more.

The Elements

Li (fire) is above Kan (water), a destructive relationship. The nuclear trigrams are just the opposite, with Kan above Li. Here the elements suggest a potentially destructive relationship that holds the promise of great success when the two elements combine to become steam, signifying power and energy.

The Moving Lines

Line 1 (at the bottom): Goals cannot be attained. There are obstacles and a series of difficulties that plague you continuously until eventually you might be sorely tempted to give up. If you do there is humiliation. If you persevere, however, there is success.

Line 2: This line suggests a certain amount of small triumphs, but only after much hard work. Do not allow yourself to be discouraged, however. Life's victories usually taste sweetest when the pursuit was hardest.

Line 3: This line indicates initial frustration that can well discourage lesser beings. Goals seems so near but yet so far. Travel will speed up the completion of your project.

Line 4: Good fortune is suggested by this line. Difficulties evaporate with unexpected help. What seemed fearful in its ability to make life tough for you now transforms into helpful energy. You have much to be thankful for.

Line 5: Proceed with confidence as good fortune brings success, promotion and helpful benefactors. You will see the successful completion of a project that is truly close to your heart. So rejoice in your good fortune and turn your thoughts to helping someone else to achieve their dreams.

Line 6: This line indicates you are presently embroiled in a complicated situation that might well ruin you. This line brings the hope that things will soon be resolved. A way out will be offered to you that will be something of a turning point. The oracle is seldom wrong in identifying turning points. Think about what this line is telling you.

Glossary

Base Hexagram
The hexagram that describes your present situation.

Changing Line
The line of the base hexagram that transforms the original hexagram into a new and predictive hexagram.

Chen
A trigram made up of two broken lines above one solid line. Chen signifies the Arousing and its element is big wood.

Chi
The life force or vital energy of the universe. Chi can be either auspicious or inauspicious.

Chien
A trigram made up of three unbroken solid lines. Chien signifies the Creative and its element is big metal.

Coin Oracle
The method of divination invented by the sage Kuei Kuo Tse. The three coin method was revised by the scholar Wang Hung Shu and is a popular method of divination in both China and the West.

Destructive Cycle
The cycle of elements in which wood devours earth, which destroys water, which kills fire, which consumes metal, which destroys wood.

Early Heaven arrangement
One of the two Pa Kua arrangements.

Elements
There are five elements in Chinese belief – earth, wood, fire, metal and water.

Feng Shui
Literally meaning 'wind/water', it is the Chinese system of balancing the energy patterns of the physical environment.

Four Pillars of Destiny
Chinese divination system of predicting life and destiny.

Hexagram
A figure made up of six lines symbolizing the universal archetypes of human consciousness. A hexagram comprises two trigrams, one placed above the other, and there are 64 hexagrams in the I Ching.

I Ching
A classic Chinese book of divination, known in the West as The *Book of Changes*. It is the major sourcebook of Feng Shui and probably the main source of most of China's cultural practices. The concepts of yin and yang, positive and negative forces and good fortune and misfortune are all derived from interpretations of the texts and judgments of the I Ching's 64 hexagrams.

Kan
A trigram made up of one solid yang line between two broken yin lines. Kan signifies the Abysmal and its and element is water.

Ken
A trigram made up of one solid yang line above two broken yin lines. Ken signifies the Mountain and its element is small earth.

Kun
A trigram made up of three broken yin lines. Kun signifies the Receptive and its element is big earth.

Later Heaven arrangement
One of the two Pa Kua arrangements.

Li
A trigram, made up of one broken yin line between two solid yang lines. Li signifies the Clinging and its element is fire.

Nuclear trigram
The hidden trigrams of any hexagram, symbolizing the underlying forces and tensions that may be clouding the situation. The lower nuclear trigram is made up of the second, third and fourth lines of the hexagram (counting from the bottom upwards). The upper nuclear trigram is made up of the third, fourth and fifth lines.

Pa Kua
An eight-sided symbol deriving its significance from the eight trigrams of the I Ching. It corresponds to the four cardinal points of the compass and the four sub-directions.

Plum Blossom Oracle
The system of I Ching divination devised by Shao Kang Chieh.

Predictive Hexagram
The hexagram that contains the predicted outcome.

Primary Trigram
The external trigrams of any hexagram, symbolizing the obvious and easily detected forces at work in the prevailing situation. The lower primary trigram is made up of the first, second and third lines of the hexagram (counting from the bottom upwards). The upper primary trigram is made up of the fourth, fifth and sixth lines.

Productive Cycle
The cycle of elements in which water feeds wood, which feeds fire, which makes earth, which in turn holds water.

Purple Star Astrology
A Chinese system of fortune telling.

Sun
A trigram made up of two solid yang lines above a single broken yin line. Sun signifies the Penetrating and its element is fire.

Tien Ti Ren
The trinity of heaven luck, earth luck and man luck.

Trigram
A figure made up of three lines, either broken or complete, symbolizing the trinity of heaven, earth and man. Trigrams are the root source of the hexagrams that make up the I Ching. There are eight trigrams in total, each with a different association.

Tui
A trigram made up of one broken yin line above two solid yang lines. Tui signifies the Joyous and its element is small metal.

Yang
Creative energy, one aspect of the complementary opposites in Chinese philosophy. It reflects the more active, moving, warmer, masculine aspects.

Yin
Receptive energy, one aspect of the complementary opposites in Chinese philosophy. It reflects the more passive, still, reflective, feminine aspects.

Index

Acknowledgements

Executive Editor David Alexander
Managing Editor Clare Churly
Editor Lesley Levene
Creative Director Tracy Killick
Designer Martin Lovelock
Illustrator Jane Evans
Production Manager Martin Croshaw

For further information, visit Lillian Too's websites.
Author website: www.lillian-too.com
Internet feng shui magazine: www.wofs.com
Feng shui Ecommerce website: www.fsmegamall.com